Desert Vegan Box Set:

2 Books in 1 with 150+

Recipes

Vegan Ice Cream Recipes

Free Gift Included

As part of our commitment to making sure you live a healthy lifestyle, we have included a free e-book in the link below. This book informs of the food groups and food items that will enable you to lose weight quickly. I hope that you enjoy this e-book and the extra gift as well. The link to the gift is below:

http://36potentfoodstoloseweightandlivehealthy.gr8.com

Disclaimer

Copyright © 2016

All Rights Reserved.

No part of this eBook can be transmitted or reproduced in any form including print, electronic, photocopying, scanning, mechanical or recording without prior written permission from the author.

While the author has taken utmost efforts to ensure the accuracy of the written content, all readers are advised to follow information mentioned herein at their own risk. The author cannot be held responsible for any personal or commercial damage caused by information. All readers are encouraged to seek professional advice when needed.

Book description

In this book, you will be introduced to a whole new world of vegan ice creams. This book is a guide for all those who are under the impression that if they follow a vegan diet, they will never get to enjoy creamy and delicious ice cream ever again. To bust that myth, this book has collated a bunch of quick and easy recipes that will tantalize your taste buds without a drop of dairy in sight!

This book is full of delicious ice cream recipes that will cause a party of flavors in your mouth, without compromising your dietary restrictions. Another good thing about the recipes in this book is that they are extremely easy to prepare and can be made in a short time; without you having to slave over the recipes for hours at a time.

When people hear the word "vegan" they have a mental picture of boring, bland and extremely tasteless food. They often think that dessert = fruit and that you need to say goodbye to the delicious ice creams that you love and cherish. This book is here to prove all the naysayers wrong. With a bunch of delicious vegan-friendly ice cream recipes, you can proudly present healthy, delicious ice creams to your family and friends.

Table of Contents

Free Gift Included 4

Disclaimer 6

Book description 8

Table of Contents 10

Introduction 21

Vegan Sorbet, Slush and Ice Recipes 24

    Vegan Peanut Butter Ice 24

    Cherry Ice Slush 26

    Strawberry Lemonade Slush 28

    Pina Colada Ice 30

    Fruit Ice 32

    Fizzy Cola Ice 34

    Lemon Sorbet 36

    Berry Sorbet 38

    Mango Sorbet 40

- Watermelon Sorbet 42
- Chocolate Sorbet 44

Vegan Ice Cream Recipes 46
- Soy Pumpkin Ice Cream 46
- Dairy Free Banana & Pecan Ice Cream 48
- Dairy Free Dark Chocolate Ice Cream 49
- Tropical Watermelon, Mango, Banana & Strawberry Ice Cream 52
- Dairy Free Banana & Peanut Butter Ice Cream 54
- Soft Serve Ice Cream 56
- Vanilla Ice Cream 57
- Strawberry Ice Cream 59
- Cantaloupe Ice Cream 61
- Fig, Coconut and Blackberry Ice Cream 63
- Coconut Ice Cream 66
- Chocolate Ice cream 68
- Mango Ice Cream 70
- Lavender Ice Cream 72
- 3 Ingredients Healthy Ice Cream 74

Salted Caramel Ice Cream 76

Peach Almond Ice Cream 79

Mint Chocolate Chip Ice Cream 81

Cherry Chunk Protein Ice Cream 84

Rose n Raspberry Ice Cream 86

Royale Nut Ice Cream 88

Berry Cheesecake Ice Cream 90

Blueberry Chocolate Chunk Ice Cream 92

Roasted Peach Ice Cream 95

Spiced Banana Walnut Ice Cream 98

Vegan Snickers Ice Cream 100

Super Fudgy Marble Fudge Ice Cream 103

Rum and Raisin Ice Cream 106

Pistachio Ice Cream 109

Swiss Almond Ice Cream 111

Vegan Sundae Sauce Recipes 114

Warm Berry Sauce 114

Hot Fudge Sundae Sauce 116

Peanut Butter Hot Fudge ... 118

Chocolate Sauce ... 120

Caramel Sauce ... 121

Sundae Recipes ... 123

Create your own Sundaes ... 123

Buster Parfait ... 125

Banana Ice Cream Sundae ... 126

Grilled Banana Split ... 128

Dairy Free Yogurt Sundae with Fruit & Chocolate Sauce ... 130

Chocolate Sundae ... 132

Triple Sundae ... 134

Conclusion ... 136

About the author ... 139

Disclaimer ... 140

Introduction ... 142

Breakfast ... 147

   1. Chocolate Chia Smoothie Pudding ... 147

   2. Thin Chocolate Crepes ... 150

3. Chocolate Hazelnut Spread 152

4. Double Chocolate Oatmeal 154

5. Brownie Breakfast Bake 156

6. Vegan Chocolate Waffles 159

7. Banana-Chocolate Chip Waffles 162

8. Chai Chocolate Oatmeal 164

9. Banana and Chocolate Porridge 167

10. Chocolate Tapioca Pudding 169

11. Chocolate French Toast 172

12. Chocolate Chip and Pumpkin Pancakes 175

Bakes and Cakes 178

13. Chocolate Mug Cake 178

14. Oatmeal and Chocolate Pie 181

15. Pumpkin Chocolate Loaf 183

16. Chocolate Chip Bagels 187

17. Chocolate Banana Bread 190

18. Chickpea Blondies 193

19. Chocolate Chip Muffins 195

20. Chocolate Chip Biscotti 198

21. Protein Donuts 200

22. Three Ingredient Brownies 202

23. Chocolate Orange Scones 204

24. Chocolate Chip Scones 207

25. Dark Chocolate Zucchini Cake 210

26. Coffee and Chocolate Muffins 213

27. Avocado Chocolate Cake 216

28. Chocolate Filled Puff Pastry 218

29. Chocolate Lava Cake 221

30. Chocolate Oreo Cheesecake 224

31. Chocolate Hazelnut Donuts 227

32. The Depression Cake 229

Cookies 232

33. Chewy Cherry Chocolate Cookies 232

34. Peanut Butter and Chocolate Macaroons 235

35. Flourless Peanut Butter Biscuits 237

36. Coconut Flour Chocolate Chip Cookies 240

37. Chocolate Quinoa Cookies 243

38. Dark Chocolate Shortbread Cookies 246

39. Chocolate Espresso Cookies 248

40. Three Ingredient Chocolate Chip Cookies 251

41. Vegan Oreos 253

Candies 256

42. Simple 3 Ingredient Chocolate Bars 256

43. Dark Chocolate Truffles 258

44. Chocolate Jelly 261

45. Jam Filled Chocolates 264

45. Pine Bark Chocolate 267

46. Chocolate Dipped Biscotti 270

47. Vegan Chocolate "Eggs" 273

48. Chocolate Covered Popcorns 276

49. White Chocolate Bar 278

50. Almond Chocolate and Cherry Crisps 280

51. Vegan Kit Kat 282

52. Chocolate Peanut Butter Cups 284

Fruits and Chocolate 287

    53. Chocolate Covered Cherries 287

    54. Raspberry Hot Chocolate 290

    55. Fruity Chocolaty Oat Bars 292

    56. Cupped Chocolate Apricot Truffles 295

    57. Chocolate Dipped Strawberries 298

    58. Chocolate Chip Filled Banana Bread Bites 300

    59. Chocolate Amoretti Peaches 302

Handy Snacks 304

    60. Chocolate Coated Raisins 304

    61. Super Balls 306

    62. Chocolate Fudge Pops 309

    63. Pumpkin Chocolate Rounds 311

    64. Chocolate Banana Bites 313

    65. Coconut Filled Chocolate Balls 315

Ice-Cream 317

    66. Mocha Ice-cream 317

    67. Peanut Butter, Banana and Chocolate Ice-Cream 320

68. Banana Split 323

Shakes and Smoothies 325

    69. Crackpot Hot Chocolate 325

    70. Mocha Ice cream Shake 327

    71. White Hot Chocolate 329

    72. Almond Avocado Chocolate Smoothie 331

    73. Chocolate Spinach Smoothie 333

    74. Cookie Dough Shake 335

    75. Cacao and Maca Smoothie 337

    76. Spicy Chocolate Smoothie 339

    77. Chocolate Raspberry Smoothie 342

    78. Chocolate and Peanut Butter Power Smoothie 344

    79. Chocolate Chip Mint Smoothie 347

    80. Almond Coconut Mocha 349

    81. Chocolate Avocado Smoothie 351

    82. Overnight Oats Smoothie 353

    83. Oreo Blizzard 354

Sauces, Syrups and Frostings 357

84. Chocolate Ganache 357

85. Chocolate Avocado Frosting... 360

86. Chocolate Fudge Sauce 362

87. Chocolate Syrup.. 364

88. Caramel Chocolate Sauce 366

89. Simple Chocolate Sauce 368

90. Chocolate Dip 370

91. Chocolate Cream "Cheese" Frosting 373

No Bake Desserts.. 376

92. Black Bean Brownie Pops 376

93. Chocolate Peppermint Mousse 378

94. Authentic Chocolate Pudding 380

95. Chocolate Chip Cookie Dough 382

96. Peanut Butter and Chocolate Tarts 384

97. Pistachio Topped Mousse 387

98. No Bake Brownies 389

99. Quick Chocolate Fudge.. 392

100. Chocolate Custard.. 394

101. Peanut Butter and Chocolate Coated Pretzels 397

Conclusion 399

Appendix 401

Introduction

People often believe that the vegan diet is extremely monotonous and restrictive. Another commonly held belief is that the diet is synonymous with bland food without much room for desserts, let alone exotic flavors! Well, these all are nothing but misguided opinions and are absolutely not true!

Firstly, let's get this straight. The vegan diet is not just a diet; it is a way of life. In other diet plans you stop eating selected foods. While following the vegan way of life, you give up on all animal based products, food or not! The first mistake people who shift to the vegan way of life make is that they jump in head first without any prior research. Take a few days and research everything that you can, and then slowly ease yourself into the diet.

Unlike a few years ago, when vegans had minimal food choices, today the food scene has completely changed. With more and more people choosing to follow the vegan way of life, companies have started to mass-produce vegan-friendly products that can make your life a lot easier (and tastier!).

One of the things that people in the past missed out on was consuming delicious and creamy ice cream while following the vegan diet. But, now, with so many dairy-free options available, life has become a lot easier for vegans! Almond milk, soy milk, soy yogurt, etc. are just some of the various dairy alternatives you can use to prepare delicious goodies, without adding unhealthy elements to your diet.

People will also try to bring you down by saying, "The vegan way of life will burn a hole through your wallet," but pay them no heed. What you spend extra here is a fraction of the cost people usually ends up paying in hospital bills due to their unhealthy diets! This book contains a bunch of delicious, healthy and vegan-friendly sorbets, ice, ice cream, sundae and sundae topping recipes that are extremely easy to make and can be prepared quickly!

I would like to take this opportunity to thank you for choosing this book and I hope it will help you add a sweet touch to your healthy vegan diet!

Vegan Sorbet, Slush and Ice Recipes

Vegan Peanut Butter Ice

| Prep: 10 min | Total: 10 min | Servings: 1 |

Ingredients

- 2 1/2 teaspoons agave nectar (can be adjusted to taste)
- 4 cups ice cubes
- 1/4 cup crunchy peanut butter (can be adjusted to taste)
- 1 cup soy milk
- 2 teaspoons carob powder (can be adjusted to taste)

Instructions

1. Place the soymilk and peanut butter together in the jar of a blender. Blitz until just combined.
2. Add in the carob powder and agave nectar and blitz for a few more minutes.
3. Finally add in the ice cubes and blend until it gets a slush like texture.
4. Pour into a margarita glass and serve immediately.
5. Enjoy!

Additional Tip

- If you do not like agave nectar, you can substitute it with stevia.

Cherry Ice Slush

| Prep: 10 min | Total: 25 min | Servings: 4 |

Ingredients

- 4 cups cherries, pitted + extra for garnishing
- 4 tablespoons cherry syrup
- 3 cups water
- 4 teaspoons vanilla extract
- 4 tablespoons sugar
- 15-20 ice cubes

Instructions

1. Add cherries, water, sugar, and cherry syrup to a heavy bottomed pot.

2. Place the pot over medium heat and simmer until cherries are cooked.

3. When done, cool slightly and blend in a blender. Transfer into a bowl.

4. Add ice cubes to a food processor and pulse until crushed.

5. Transfer crushed into glasses.

6. Pour blended cherry over it.

7. Garnish with cherries and serve immediately.

8. Enjoy!

Strawberry Lemonade Slush

| Prep: 10 min | Total: 12 min | Servings: 2 |

Ingredients

- 1 cup fresh strawberries, chopped roughly
- Zest of 1/2 lemon
- Juice of 1 lemon
- 2-3 tablespoons sugar or to taste
- 1 1/2 cups water
- 1 cup ice cubes

Instructions

1. Add all the ingredients except ice to a blender and blend until smooth.

2. Finally add in the ice cubes and blend until it gets a slush like texture.

3. Pour into 2 tall glasses and serve immediately.

4. Enjoy!

Pina Colada Ice

| Prep: 5 min | Total: 5 min | Servings: 6 |

Instructions

- 1 cup canned pineapple juice
- 2 frozen bananas, chopped
- 4 cups fresh pineapple pieces
- 1 cup coconut milk
- 2 cups crushed ice

Instructions

1. Add all the ingredients except ice to a blender and blend until smooth.

2. Finally add in the ice cubes and blend until it gets a slush like texture.

3. Pour into 4 margarita glasses and serve immediately.

4. Enjoy!

Fruit Ice

| Prep: 2 min | Total: 2 min | Servings: 2 |

Ingredients

- 1 cup fruit juice of your choice
- 2 cups crushed ice

Instructions

1. Add juice ice to a blender and blend until it gets a slush like texture.
2. Pour into 2 tall glasses and serve immediately.
3. Enjoy!

Fizzy Cola Ice

| Prep: 5 min | Total: 5 min | Servings: 4 |

Ingredients

- 3 cups snow
- 18 ounces cola-flavored carbonated beverage

Instructions

1. Combine the snow and the carbonated cola in a large bowl. Mix well by hand.
2. Spoon into a serving bowl or a tall glass and serve immediately.
3. Enjoy!

Lemon Sorbet

| Prep: 5 min | Total: 2 hrs. 25 min | Servings: 8 |

Ingredients

- 3 cups fresh lemon juice, passed through a sieve
- 2 cups sugar
- 1/4 teaspoon salt
- 2 cups sugar

Instructions

1. Place a saucepan over medium heat. Add water and sugar and cook until sugar dissolves.
2. Remove from heat and cool for a while. Add lemon juice and salt.

3. Mix, cover and refrigerate overnight.
4. Pour the lemonade mix into an ice cream churner and follow the manufacturer's instructions to freeze for 15-20 minutes.
5. When churned, pour into a freezer-safe container and place in the freezer and freeze until firm.
6. Scoop out using a scooper dipped in warm water and serve in bowls immediately.
7. Enjoy!

Berry Sorbet

| Prep: 10 min | Total: 4 hrs. 30 min | Servings: 8 |

Ingredients

- 1 1/2 pounds strawberries / raspberries / blueberries / blackberries
- Juice of a lemon
- 1/3 cup maple syrup

Instructions

1. Blend together berries and lemon juice until smooth.
2. Pass the blended berries through a fine sieve. Discard the solids and seeds.

3. Add maple syrup to the blended berries. Mix well, cover and chill for 30 minutes.
4. Pour the mixture into an ice cream churner and follow the manufacturer's instructions to freeze for 15-20 minutes.
5. When churned, pour into a freezer-safe container and place in the freezer and freeze until firm.
6. Transfer the churned mixture into a freezer-safe container, cover and freeze for 3-4 hours
7. Scoop out using a scooper dipped in warm water and serve in bowls immediately.
8. Enjoy!

Mango Sorbet

| Prep: 10 min | Total: 1 hr. 45 min | Servings: 8-10 |

Ingredients

- 4 cup ripe mango, chopped
- 1 1/2 cups white sugar or to taste
- 2 cups water

Instructions

1. Place a saucepan over medium heat. Add water and sugar and cook until sugar dissolves.
2. Remove from heat and cool for a while.
3. Blend together mangoes and sugar solution until smooth.

4. Pour the mixture into an ice cream churner and follow the manufacturer's instructions to freeze for 15-20 minutes
5. When churned, pour into a freezer-safe container and place in the freezer and freeze for an hour.
6. Scoop out using a scooper dipped in warm water and serve in bowls immediately.
7. Enjoy!

Watermelon Sorbet

Prep: 15 min	Total: 1 hr. 45 min	Servings: 4-6

Ingredients

- 3 cups watermelon, deseeded, chopped
- 1/4 cup sugar
- 1/4 cup water
- Juice of a lemon

Instructions

1. Place a saucepan over medium heat. Add water and sugar and cook until sugar dissolves.
2. Remove from heat and cool for a while.
3. Blend together watermelon and sugar solution until smooth.

4. Chill for about an hour.
5. Pour the mixture into an ice cream churner and follow the manufacturer's instructions to freeze for 15-20 minutes
6. When churned, pour into a freezer-safe container and place in the freezer and freeze for an hour.
7. Scoop out using a scooper dipped in warm water and serve in bowls immediately.
8. Enjoy!

Chocolate Sorbet

| Prep: 15 min | Total: 1 hr. 45 min | Servings: 8-10 |

Ingredients

- 2 cups vegan dark chocolate chips
- 4 cups water
- 1/2 cup agave nectar

Instructions

1. Place a saucepan over medium heat. Add water and agave and cook until agave dissolves.
2. Remove from heat and add chocolate chips and mix until chips are melted. Cool for a while.
3. Blend in a blender until smooth.

4. Chill for about an hour.

5. Pour the mixture into an ice cream churner and follow the manufacturer's instructions to freeze for 15-20 minutes.

6. When churned, pour into a freezer-safe container and place in the freezer and freeze for an hour.

7. Scoop out using a scooper dipped in warm water and serve in bowls immediately.

8. Enjoy!

Vegan Ice Cream Recipes

Soy Pumpkin Ice Cream

Prep: 10 min	Total: 3 h 50 min	Servings: 8

Ingredients

- 1 tablespoon pumpkin pie spice
- 1/2 cup soy creamer
- 3 1/2 cups soy creamer
- 1/4 cup arrowroot powder
- 2 cups soy milk
- 2 cups pumpkin puree
- 1 1/2 cups brown sugar
- 2 teaspoons vanilla extract

Instructions

1. Pour the arrowroot powder into 1/4 cup of soy creamer. Mix well and keep aside.
2. Pour the 3-½ cups of soy creamer into a large saucepan. Slowly heat it up over a medium flame and add in the soymilk, pumpkin puree, brown sugar, vanilla extract and pumpkin spice mix. Whisk well using a wire whisk until the mix starts bubbling around the edges.
3. Take the saucepan off the heat and set aside for about 30 to 45 minutes or until cooled to room temperature.
4. Pour the cooled ice cream mix into an ice cream churner and follow the manufacturer's instructions to freeze the ice cream.
5. Scoop out using a scooper dipped in warm water and serve immediately.
6. Enjoy!

Dairy Free Banana & Pecan Ice Cream

| Prep: 10 min | Total: 10 min | Servings: 4 |

Ingredients

- 4 large frozen bananas, cut into small chunks
- 2 tablespoons chopped pecans
- 2 cups unsweetened almond milk
- 2 pinches ground cinnamon, or to taste

Instructions

1. Place the banana chunks, chopped pecans, cinnamon and almond milk in the jar of a blender or food processor.
2. Blend until it gets a smooth creamy texture.
3. Spoon into a serving bowl and serve immediately.
4. Enjoy!

Dairy Free Dark Chocolate Ice Cream

Prep: 15 min	Total: 8 h 30 min	Servings: 4

Ingredients

- 1 teaspoon vanilla sugar
- 3 1/2 ounces dark chocolate, chopped
- 1/4 teaspoon xanthan gum
- 1 3/4 teaspoons aquafaba
- 1/4 cup confectioners' sugar

Instructions

1. Heat a pot of water on high flame. Once it is boiling, lower the flame until the water is simmering and place a double boiler over, ensuring that the bottom of the double boiler vessel doesn't touch the surface of the water.

2. Place the dark chocolate in the double boiler and melt, stirring constantly and scraping the sides using a rubber spatula. This will ensure that the chocolate doesn't scorch.
3. Once the chocolate has melted completely, take the double boiler vessel off the pot with water and let it cool to room temperature.
4. Fix a stand mixer with a whisk attachment.
5. In the bowl of the stand mixer, add the aquafaba and whisk it on high speed until the aquafaba becomes light and fluffy and is about 4 times its original volume.
6. Add in the xanthan gum and whisk for about 30 seconds more.
7. Add in the vanilla sugar and confectioner's sugar and whisk for another 2 minutes or until the mix has a glossy sheen and is firm.
8. Add in the melted chocolate and mix using the cut and fold method until the chocolate is well incorporated.
9. Transfer the prepared ice cream into a freezer-safe container.

10. Freeze for a minimum 8 hours or overnight.

11. Scoop with a scooper dipped in warm water and scoop into a serving bowl.

12. Serve immediately.

13. Enjoy!

Tropical Watermelon, Mango, Banana & Strawberry Ice Cream

| Prep: 10 min | Total: 10 min | Servings: 4 |

Ingredients

- 2 bananas, cut into large chunks and frozen
- 1 cup mango chunks, frozen
- 2 cups watermelon, diced and frozen
- 1/2 cup almonds, slivered (optional)
- 1/2 cup strawberries, frozen
- 2 teaspoons hemp seeds, or to taste (optional)

Instructions

1. Place the frozen banana chunks, frozen mango chunks, frozen watermelon chunks and frozen strawberries in the jar of the blender. Blend until smooth.

2. If using hemp seeds; add them to the blender and blend until well mixed.

3. Pour the prepared ice cream into a freezer-safe bowl. Add in the slivered almonds and mix by hand.

4. Scoop with a scooper dipped in warm water and serve immediately or freeze until ready to eat.

5. Enjoy!

Dairy Free Banana & Peanut Butter Ice Cream

Prep: 15 min	Total: 15 min	Servings: 6

Ingredients

- 1/4 cup vanilla soy milk
- 8 bananas, sliced and frozen
- 1 teaspoon vanilla extract
- 1/2 cup peanut butter
- 1 teaspoon ground cinnamon

Instructions

1. Place the frozen banana slices, vanilla extract, peanut butter and cinnamon in the jar of a food processor.
2. Blend until smooth, making sure to pause once every 30 seconds to scrape down the sides of the jar using a spatula.

3. Slowly pour in the soymilk and keep blending until it forms a smooth mix.

4. Scoop into a serving bowl and serve immediately.

5. Enjoy!

Soft Serve Ice Cream

| Prep: 5 min | Total: 7 min | Servings: 6 |

Ingredients

- 6 bananas, peeled, sliced, frozen
- 2 teaspoons vanilla extract
- 1/3 cup nondairy milk like soy / almond / rice etc

Instructions

1. Blend together all the ingredients until smooth and creamy. Add a little more milk if required, a tablespoon at a time.
2. Scoop into a serving bowl and serve immediately.
3. Enjoy!

Vanilla Ice Cream

| Prep: 5 min | Total: 35 min | Servings: 3 |

Ingredients

- 1/2 cup almond milk
- 3/4 cup full-fat coconut milk, chilled (use only the fat which is floating on top)
- 1 1/2 - 2 tablespoons white sugar
- 1 tablespoon vanilla extract
- 1/8 teaspoon salt

Instructions

1. Place milk, sugar, vanilla and salt in the food processor jar. Blend until smooth.

2. Pour the mixture into an ice cream churner and follow the manufacturer's instructions to freeze the ice cream or pour into a freezer safe container and place in the freezer. Whisk every 30 minutes until ice cream is frozen.
3. Scoop out using a scooper dipped in warm water and serve immediately.
4. Enjoy!

Strawberry Ice Cream

| Prep: 5 min | Total: 4 hrs. 5 min | Servings: 3-4 |

Ingredients

- 1 cup coconut cream or full fat coconut milk
- 1/2 teaspoon vanilla extract
- 3/4 pound frozen strawberries
- 2-3 tablespoons pure maple syrup
- A pinch salt

Instructions

1. Place all the ingredients in the food processor jar. Blend until smooth.
2. Pour into a freezer-safe container and place in the freezer. Freeze for 4 hours or until ice cream is frozen.

3. Remove from the freezer at least 10-15 minutes before serving.

4. Scoop out using a scooper dipped in warm water and serve.

5. Enjoy!

Cantaloupe Ice Cream

| Prep: 15 min | Total: 45 min | Servings: 8 |

Ingredients

- 1 1/2 pounds chilled, cantaloupe, peeled, deseeded, chopped into cubes
- 3/4 cup canned coconut milk, chilled
- 1 1/3 cups sugar or to taste
- 1 1/2 cups chilled water

Instructions

1. Add cantaloupe pieces to a blender and blend until smooth. Transfer into a large bowl.
2. Whisk together coconut milk and sugar until it becomes slightly thick.

3. Add coconut cream mixture to cantaloupe and whisk until well combined.

4. Pour the mixture into an ice cream churner for 30 minutes and follow the manufacturer's instructions to freeze the ice cream or pour into a freezer safe container and place in the freezer. Whisk every 30 minutes until ice cream is frozen.

5. Scoop out using a scooper dipped in warm water and serve immediately.

6. Enjoy!

Fig, Coconut and Blackberry Ice Cream

Prep: 5 min	Total: 60 min	Servings: 4

Ingredients

- 1/3 cup blackberries + extra to garnish
- 5 fresh, ripe figs, chopped
- 1 cup coconut milk
- 3 tablespoons water
- 3 tablespoons dried shredded coconut, unsweetened
- 4-5 tablespoons agave nectar or to taste
- 2 teaspoons lemon juice
- Zest of 1/2 lemon, grated
- 1/2 teaspoon ginger, minced (optional)

Instructions

1. Place a saucepan over medium heat.
2. Add water, lemon zest, dried coconut and ginger. Bring to a boil.
3. Simmer until figs are tender.
4. Add blackberries and agave and cook until slightly thick (like jam)
5. Remove from heat and cool completely and add to a blender.
6. Add rest of the ingredients and pulse for a few seconds such that fruits get chopped into tiny pieces.
7. Pour the mixture into an ice cream churner for 30 minutes and follow the manufacturer's instructions to freeze the ice cream or pour into a freezer safe container and place in the freezer. Whisk every 30 minutes until ice cream is frozen.
8. Scoop out using a scooper dipped in warm water and serve immediately garnished with blackberries.
9. Enjoy!

Coconut Ice Cream

| Prep: 5 min | Total: 5 hrs. | Servings: 3-4 |

Ingredients

- 1 can (15 ounces) full fat coconut milk, divided
- 3 teaspoons cornstarch
- 6 tablespoons sugar
- 2 tablespoons dried, shredded coconut, unsweetened, toasted (optional)

Instructions

1. Whisk together in a small bowl, 2-3 tablespoons coconut milk and cornstarch and set aside.
2. Add rest of the ingredients to a heavy bottomed pan and place the pan over medium heat.

3. When it begins to simmer, add cornstarch mixture stirring constantly.
4. Continue stirring until the mixture thickens.
5. Remove from heat and cool completely. Cover and chill for 4 hours.
6. Pour the mixture into an ice cream churner for 30 minutes and follow the manufacturer's instructions to freeze the ice cream or pour into a freezer safe container and place in the freezer. Whisk every 30 minutes until ice cream is frozen.
7. Scoop out using a scooper dipped in warm water and serve garnished with toasted coconut if using.
8. Enjoy!

Chocolate Ice cream

| Prep: 3 min | Total: 4 hrs. 30 min | Servings: 3-4 |

Ingredients

- 1 can (15 ounces) full-fat coconut milk
- 1/4 cup cocoa powder, unsweetened
- 1/2 cup sugar or to taste

Instructions

1. Place a heavy bottomed pan over medium heat.
2. Add all the ingredients and simmer for around 8 minutes.
3. Remove from heat and cool completely. Cover and chill for 4 hours.
4. Pour the mixture into an ice cream churner for 15-20 minutes and follow the manufacturer's instructions to freeze the ice

cream or pour into a freezer safe container and place in the freezer. Whisk every 30 minutes until ice cream is frozen.

5. Scoop out using a scooper dipped in warm water and serve.
6. Enjoy!

Mango Ice Cream

| Prep: 7 min | Total: 4 hrs. 40 min | Servings: 10 |

Ingredients

- 3 cups ripe mango, chopped
- 2 cans (14 ounces each) full-fat coconut milk, unsweetened
- 1 cup almond milk
- 1 cup organic evaporated cane sugar
- 1 teaspoon vanilla extract
- 2 tablespoons orange liqueur

Instructions

1. Place all the ingredients in the food processor jar. Blend until smooth.

2. Transfer into a container, cover and chill for 3-4 hours.
3. Pour the mixture into an ice cream churner for 15-20 minutes and follow the manufacturer's instructions to freeze the ice cream or pour into a freezer safe container and place in the freezer. Freeze for 4 hours or until ice cream is frozen.
4. Remove from the freezer at least 10-15 minutes before serving.
5. Scoop out using a scooper dipped in warm water and serve.
6. Enjoy!

Lavender Ice Cream

| Prep: 5 min | Total: 4 hrs. 25 min | Servings: 4 |

Ingredients

- 4 tablespoons edible lavender flowers
- 2 cups full-fat coconut milk
- 4 bananas, peeled, chopped, frozen
- 4 tablespoons maple syrup or to taste

Instructions

1. Place a heavy bottomed pan over medium heat.
2. Add coconut milk and lavender.
3. When it begins to boil, remove from heat. Cover and set aside for 30-35 minutes.
4. Strain the mixture and discard lavender flowers.

5. Pour into a freezer-safe container and place in the freezer. Freeze for 4 hours or until ice cream is frozen.

6. Chop the frozen ice cream and add to a food processor. Add bananas and maple syrup and pulse until smooth and creamy. At this stage, the ice cream is a soft serve ice cream. If you do not like soft serve, freeze for an hour.

7. Scoop out using a scooper dipped in warm water and serve.

8. Enjoy!

3 Ingredients Healthy Ice Cream

| Prep: 5 min | Total: 25 min | Servings: 8 |

Ingredients

- 1 cup coconut milk, divided
- 3 cups fresh fruit juice of your choice
- 3 tablespoons cornstarch or tapioca starch

Instructions

1. Mix together in a bowl cornstarch and 3-4 tablespoons coconut milk and set aside.
2. Pour the remaining coconut milk in a heavy bottomed pan and place the pan over low heat.
3. When it starts simmering, add cornstarch mixture stirring constantly. Continue stirring until the mixture thickens.

4. Remove from heat.

5. Add juice and whisk. Transfer into a bowl and cool completely.

6. Refrigerate for a few hours until chilled.

7. Pour the mixture into an ice cream churner for 15-20 minutes and follow the manufacturer's instructions to freeze the ice cream or pour into a freezer safe container and place in the freezer. Freeze for 4 hours or until ice cream is frozen.

8. Remove from the freezer at least 10-15 minutes before serving.

9. Scoop out using a scooper dipped in warm water and serve.

10. Enjoy!

Salted Caramel Ice Cream

| Prep: 10 min | Total: 2 hrs. 40 min | Servings: 4 |

Ingredients

For salted caramel

- 6 tablespoons coconut sugar
- 4 tablespoons full-fat coconut milk
- 1 tablespoon maple syrup
- 1/2 teaspoon vanilla extract
- 1/8 teaspoon sea salt

For ice cream:

- 6 ounces firm silken tofu

- 1 teaspoon guar gum
- 50 drops liquid stevia or to taste
- 1/2 can light coconut milk
- 1/8 teaspoon sea salt

Instructions

1. To make salted caramel: Add all the ingredients to a saucepan and place over medium heat.
2. Stir constantly and bring to a boil.
3. Remove from heat and cool completely. Transfer to a bowl, cover and chill for a few hours.
4. Blend together tofu, salted caramel, coconut milk and salt until smooth.
5. Add guar gum and blend until smooth.
6. Pour the mixture into an ice cream churner for 15-20 minutes and follow the manufacturer's instructions to freeze the ice

cream or pour into a freezer safe container and place in the freezer. Freeze for 4 hours or until ice cream is frozen.

7. Remove from the freezer at least 10-15 minutes before serving.

8. Scoop out using a scooper dipped in warm water and serve.

9. Enjoy!

Peach Almond Ice Cream

| Prep: 10 min | Total: 4 hrs. 10 min | Servings: 8 |

Ingredients

- 2 cups almonds, soaked overnight
- 10 dates, pitted, chopped
- 8 peaches, pitted, chopped
- 2 cups water
- 2 teaspoons lemon juice
- 1/2 teaspoon vanilla extract
- 8 drops stevia or to taste

Instructions

1. Drain almonds and add to a blender. Add water and blend until smooth. Strain the almond milk thus obtained. Discard the unstrained part.
2. Pour it back into the blender. Add rest of the ingredients and blend until smooth.
3. Pour the mixture into an ice cream churner for 15-20 minutes and follow the manufacturer's instructions to freeze the ice cream or pour into a freezer safe container and place in the freezer. Freeze for 4 hours or until ice cream is frozen.
4. Remove from the freezer at least 10-15 minutes before serving.
5. Scoop out using a scooper dipped in warm water and serve.
6. Enjoy!

Mint Chocolate Chip Ice Cream

| Prep: 15 min | Total: 45 min | Servings: 3 |

Ingredients

- 1 1/2 cans (400 ml each) coconut milk, chilled for at least 3-4 hours
- 1/2 cup maple syrup
- 1 cup baby spinach
- 5 tablespoons dairy free chocolate chips
- 1/2 tablespoons coconut flour
- 3/4 tablespoon peppermint extract

Instructions

1. Blend spinach in a blender with about a tablespoon or two of water until smooth.
2. Pour into a small saucepan. Place the saucepan over medium heat. Cook until thick. Remove from heat and cool completely.
3. Remove the coconut milk from the refrigerator. Remove the fat that is floating on the top and add the spinach. Discard the remaining liquid of the coconut milk.
4. Add coconut flour and whisk well using an electric mixer.
5. Add remaining ingredients except for chocolate chips and whisk until smooth and creamy. Add chocolate chips and stir.
6. Pour the mixture into an ice cream churner for 15-20 minutes and follow the manufacturer's instructions to freeze the ice cream or pour into a freezer safe container and place in the freezer. Freeze for 4 hours or until ice cream is frozen.
7. Remove from the freezer at least 10-15 minutes before serving.
8. Scoop out using a scooper dipped in warm water and serve.
9. Enjoy!

Cherry Chunk Protein Ice Cream

| Prep: 10 min | Total: 50 min | Servings: 8 |

Ingredients

- 4 cups cooked navy beans
- 16 frozen strawberries, thawed, chopped
- 1 cup cherries, pitted
- 2 ripe bananas
- 4 cups vanilla hemp milk or almond milk
- 4 teaspoons vanilla extract
- 1/2 teaspoon pure almond extract
- 4 tablespoons coconut nectar

Instructions

1. Blend together navy beans, milk, banana, coconut nectar, vanilla and almond extracts until smooth and creamy. Transfer into a bowl.
2. Add strawberries and cherries.
3. Pour the mixture into an ice cream churner for 25-30 minutes and follow the manufacturer's instructions to freeze the ice cream or pour into a freezer safe container and place in the freezer. Freeze for 4 hours or until ice cream is frozen. Whisk every 30 minutes.
4. Remove from the freezer at least 10-15 minutes before serving.
5. Scoop out using a scooper dipped in warm water and serve.
6. Enjoy!

Rose n Raspberry Ice Cream

| Prep: 10 min | Total: 2 hrs. 20 min | Servings: 4 |

Ingredients

- 2 bananas, peeled, sliced, frozen
- 1 cup full fat coconut milk or coconut cream
- 1/2 cup frozen raspberries
- 3 tablespoons agave nectar
- 2 teaspoons rose water

Instructions

1. Add bananas to a food processor and pulse for a few seconds.
2. Add raspberries and rose water and blend again for a few seconds.

3. With the food processor running, add coconut milk a little at a time and continue blending until all the coconut milk is added.
4. Freeze for 2 hours.
5. Scoop out using a scooper dipped in warm water and serve.
6. Enjoy!

Royale Nut Ice Cream

| Prep: 10 min | Total: 1 hr. 10 min | Servings: 3 |

Ingredients

- 1 cup almond milk
- 6 tablespoons creamy peanut butter
- 1 tablespoon cornstarch
- 1/3 cup maple syrup
- 1/4 teaspoon salt
- 2 tablespoons pecans, finely chopped, toasted
- 1/8 teaspoon almond extract

Instructions

1. Add all the ingredients except pecans to a saucepan and whisk until well combined.
2. Place the saucepan over medium heat and stir constantly until the mixture thickens.
3. Remove from heat and cool completely.
4. Cover and chill for 2 - 3 hours in the refrigerator.
5. Pour the mixture into an ice cream churner for 25-30 minutes and follow the manufacturer's instructions to freeze the ice cream. Add pecans during the last 5 minutes of churning or pour into a freezer safe container and place in the freezer. Freeze for 4 hours or until ice cream is frozen. Whisk every 30 minutes.
6. Remove from the freezer at least 10-15 minutes before serving.
7. Scoop out using a scooper dipped in warm water and serve.
8. Enjoy!

Berry Cheesecake Ice Cream

| Prep: 20 min | Total: 3 hrs. 20 min | Servings: 8 |

Ingredients

For cheesecake Ice Cream:

- 2 cups almond milk
- 2 cups cashews, soaked in water overnight, drained
- 2 cups coconut cream or full-fat coconut milk
- 2/3 cup soft dates, pitted
- 1/2 cup maple syrup or organic granulated cane sugar
- 1/2 cup coconut oil, melted or olive oil
- 2 teaspoons vanilla extract
- Juice of a lemon

- 1 tablespoon apple cider vinegar
- 1/8 teaspoon salt

For berry swirl:

- 2 cups frozen berries of your choice like blueberry, raspberry, strawberry, blackberry
- 2 teaspoons cornstarch mixed with 2-3 teaspoons water
- 4 tablespoons maple syrup

Instructions

1. To make cheesecake ice cream: Add all the ingredients of the ice cream to a blender and blend until smooth and creamy.
2. Pour the mixture into an ice cream churner for 30-45 minutes and follow the manufacturer's instructions to freeze the ice cream or pour into a freezer safe container and place in the freezer. Freeze for 2 hours or until ice cream is semi-frozen. Whisk every 30 minutes.

3. To make berry swirl: Place a saucepan over medium-high heat. Add 1 1/2 cup berries and maple syrup. Let it simmer for a while. Mash it with the back of a spoon while it cooks.
4. Add cornstarch mixture and stir constantly until the sauce thickens. Remove from heat and add remaining berries. Transfer to a bowl, cover and refrigerate until use.
5. Add the soft churned or semi-frozen ice cream to a loaf pan. Pour the berry mixture and slightly fold in with a spatula so that a swirl effect is visible.
6. Cover and freeze for a couple of hours until set.
7. Remove from the freezer at least 10-15 minutes before serving.
8. Scoop out using a scooper dipped in warm water and serve.

Blueberry Chocolate Chunk Ice Cream

Prep: 5 min	Total: 2 hrs. 50 min	Servings: 4

Ingredients

- 1/2 cup blueberries
- 1 1/2 cups coconut milk
- 1/3 cup evaporated cane juice
- 1 tablespoon cocoa powder
- 1/4 cup bittersweet chocolate chunks
- 1 teaspoon vanilla extract

Instructions

1. Add all the ingredients except chocolate chunks to a blender and blend until smooth and creamy.
2. Pour the mixture into an ice cream churner for 30-45 minutes and follow the manufacturer's instructions to freeze the ice cream or pour into a freezer safe container and place in the freezer. Freeze for 4 hours or until ice cream is semi-frozen. Whisk every 30 minutes.

3. Transfer into a freezer-proof container with a lid. Add chocolate chunks and fold.

4. Freeze for about 2 hours.

5. Remove from the freezer at least 10-15 minutes before serving.

6. Scoop out using a scooper dipped in warm water and serve.

7. Enjoy!

Roasted Peach Ice Cream

| Prep: 10 min | Total: 1 hr. 10 min | Servings: 4 |

Ingredients

For peach puree

- 4 - 6 ripe peaches, pitted, sliced
- 4 tablespoons maple syrup
- 2 tablespoons coconut oil

For ice cream:

- 3 cups vanilla flavored coconut milk
- 3 cups full-fat coconut milk, chilled overnight

- 1/2 teaspoon ground cinnamon
- 2/3 cup maple syrup

Instructions

1. Place peach slices in a baking dish. Add coconut oil and maple syrup and mix well.
2. Bake in a preheated oven at 375 degrees F for about 20-25 minutes.
3. Remove from the oven, cool and refrigerate for 4-5 hours.
4. Remove from the refrigerator and blend until smooth.
5. Add all the ingredients to the ice cream to a bowl. Add pureed peach and whisk well.
6. Pour the mixture into an ice cream churner for 25-30 minutes and follow the manufacturer's instructions to freeze the ice cream or pour into a freezer safe container and place in the freezer. Freeze for 4 hours or until ice cream is frozen. Whisk every 30 minutes.

7. Remove from the freezer at least 10-15 minutes before serving.

8. Scoop out using a scooper dipped in warm water and serve.

9. Enjoy!

Spiced Banana Walnut Ice Cream

| Prep: 15 min | Total: 8 hrs. 20 min | Servings: 4 |

Ingredients

- 2 large bananas, peeled, chopped, frozen
- 2 cups walnuts, chopped + extra to top
- 4 soft dates, pitted, chopped
- 1 teaspoon ground cinnamon
- 2/3 teaspoon vanilla seeds
- 2 tablespoons chia seeds
- 1/8 teaspoon ground nutmeg
- 2 tablespoons cacao nibs + extra to top
- 2 tablespoons coconut oil

Instructions

1. Add walnuts to a blender and pulse for 10-15 seconds.
2. Add rest of the ingredients and blend until smooth and creamy.
3. Transfer into a freezer safe bowl with a lid and add chia seeds and cacao nibs. Mix with a spoon.
4. Sprinkle walnuts and cacao nibs. Cover and freeze overnight.

Vegan Snickers Ice Cream

| Prep: 30 min | Total: 7 hrs. | Servings: 4 |

Ingredients

- 1 3/4 cup full fat coconut milk
- 1/4 cup vegan caramel sauce
- 3 tablespoons peanuts, roasted, salted
- 1/4 cup sugar or to taste
- A pinch xanthan gum (optional)
- 1/2 teaspoon vanilla extract
- 1-ounce vegan dark chocolate, grated

Instructions

1. Place a saucepan over medium heat. Add coconut milk, sugar and bring to a boil stirring constantly until sugar dissolves completely.
2. Remove from heat and add vanilla and xanthan gum. Whisk well.
3. Transfer to a bowl, cover, and refrigerate for 6 hours.
4. Pour the mixture into an ice cream churner for 25-30 minutes and follow the manufacturer's instructions to freeze the ice cream. After 20 minutes of churning, add half the caramel sauce, half the chocolate and half the peanuts and continue churning or pour into a freezer safe container and place in the freezer. Freeze for 4 hours or until ice cream is frozen. Whisk every 30 minutes. Add caramel sauce after 3 hours of freezing.
5. After churning, transfer into a freezer-safe container. Garnish with remaining chocolate, peanuts and caramel. Fold slightly with a knife to get the look of the swirl. Freeze for 2 hours.
6. Remove from the freezer at least 10-15 minutes before serving.

7. Scoop out using a scooper dipped in warm water and serve.

8. Enjoy!

Super Fudgy Marble Fudge Ice Cream

| Prep: 15 min | Total: 3 hrs. | Servings: 4 |

Ingredients

For ice cream:

- 1/2 a 15 ounces can light coconut milk
- 1/2 a 15 ounces can regular coconut milk
- 1/2 tablespoon vanilla extract
- 1/3 cup coconut nectar
- 1/8 teaspoon xanthan gum (optional)
- 1/8 teaspoon salt

For fudgy ganache swirl:

- 1/4 cup coconut milk
- 1/2 cup vegan dark chocolate chips

Instructions

1. Make fudgy ganache as follows: Place a saucepan over medium heat. Add coconut milk and bring to a boil.
2. Remove from heat and pour into a bowl. Add chocolate chips and stir until well combined. Cool completely and set aside.
3. To make ice cream: Add all the ingredients to a blender and blend until smooth.
4. Pour into a bowl, cover and chill for a couple of hours.
5. Pour the mixture into an ice cream churner for 25-30 minutes and follow the manufacturer's instructions to freeze the ice cream or pour into a freezer safe container and place in the freezer. Freeze for 2 hours or until ice cream is semi-frozen. Whisk every 30 minutes.

6. After churning, place about 2-3 scoops of ice cream in a freezer-safe container. Take a little ganache and pour in a thin stream over the scoops. Place 2-3 more scoops of ice cream and pour remaining ganache on top. Take a butter knife and fold lightly to create a marble look. Place in the freezer for 2-3 hours.
7. Remove from the freezer at least 10-15 minutes before serving.
8. Scoop out using a scooper dipped in warm water and serve.
9. Enjoy!

Rum and Raisin Ice Cream

| Prep: 15 min | Total: 5 hrs. | Servings: 3-4 |

Ingredients

- 1 1/2 cups coconut milk, divided
- 1/3 cup raisins
- 6 tablespoons brown sugar
- 1/2 teaspoon vanilla extract
- 1 tablespoon arrowroot powder or cornstarch
- 4-5 tablespoons rum or to taste

Instructions

1. Add 2-3 tablespoons milk to a small bowl. Add arrowroot and whisk well. Set aside.

2. Place rum and raisins in a bowl and let it soak for at least 25-30 minutes.

3. Add remaining coconut milk and sugar to a saucepan. Place the saucepan over medium heat and bring to a boil. Stir constantly until sugar dissolves.

4. Remove from heat and add arrowroot mixture stirring constantly.

5. Continue stirring constantly and simmer until mixture thickens. Remove from heat.

6. Pour into a bowl, cover and chill for a couple of hours.

7. Pour the mixture into an ice cream churner for 25-30 minutes and follow the manufacturer's instructions to freeze the ice cream. Add raisins along with rum during the last minute of churning or pour into a freezer safe container and place in the freezer. Freeze for 4 hours or until ice cream is frozen. Whisk every 30 minutes. Add rum and raisins during the last time of whisking.

8. Pour the churned mixture in a freezer safe container. Cover and freeze for 2 hours.

9. Remove from the freezer at least 10-15 minutes before serving.

10. Scoop out using a scooper dipped in warm water and serve.

11. Enjoy!

Pistachio Ice Cream

| Prep: 10 min | Total: 45 min | Servings: 3-4 |

Ingredients

- 1 cup cashews, soaked overnight, drained
- 1/2 cup pistachio, shelled, unsalted, divided
- 1/2 a 15 ounces can full-fat coconut milk
- 3 tablespoons coconut oil, melted
- 6 tablespoons granulated sugar
- 1/8 teaspoon salt
- 1 teaspoon almond extract

Instructions

1. Finely powder about 1/3 cup of pistachio nuts.

2. Add milk, sugar, oil, almond extract and salt to a blender and blend until smooth and creamy.
3. Add powdered pistachio and blend again.
4. Pour the mixture into an ice cream churner for 25-30 minutes and follow the manufacturer's instructions to freeze the ice cream or pour into a freezer safe container and place in the freezer. Freeze for 4 hours or until ice cream is frozen. Whisk every 30 minutes.
5. Remove from the freezer at least 10-15 minutes before serving.
6. Scoop out using a scooper dipped in warm water and serve.
7. Enjoy!

Swiss Almond Ice Cream

Prep: 10 min	Total: 3 hrs.	Servings: 3-4

Ingredients

For chocolate covered almonds

- 1/4 cup vegan dark chocolate chips
- 1/2 cup whole raw almonds
- 1/8 teaspoon fine grain sea salt

For ice cream:

- 3/4 cup almond milk / cashew milk/ hemp milk
- 1/4 cup soft dates, pitted, chopped
- 1/8 teaspoon almond extract

- 1/2 tablespoon vanilla extract
- 1/4 teaspoon guar gum (optional)

Instructions

1. To make chocolate covered almonds: Place almonds on a baking sheet. Bake in a preheated oven at 350 degrees F for about 12 minutes.
2. Place chocolate chips and salt in a bowl. Transfer the hot, toasted almonds into the chocolate chips bowl and mix. Cover and set aside for 5 minutes. In 5 minutes, the chocolates would have melted. Mix again and place on a lined baking sheet. Refrigerate until use.
3. Blend together coconut milk and dates until smooth. Add milk, vanilla, almond extract and guar gum if using and blend until smooth.
4. Pour the mixture into an ice cream churner for 25-30 minutes and follow the manufacturer's instructions to freeze the ice

cream or pour into a freezer safe container and place in the freezer. Freeze for 4 hours or until ice cream is frozen. Whisk every 30 minutes.

5. Add churned ice cream to a freezer-safe container. Chop the chilled nuts and add to the ice cream. Stir and freeze for a couple of hours.

6. Remove from the freezer at least 10-15 minutes before serving.

7. Scoop out using a scooper dipped in warm water and serve.

8. Enjoy!

Vegan Sundae Sauce Recipes

Warm Berry Sauce

| Prep: 5 min | Total: 20 min | Servings: 10 |

Ingredients

- 1/2 cup water
- 1 cup berries of your choice like raspberries, blueberries, strawberries or a mixture of berries, fresh or frozen

Instructions

1. Add berries and water to a saucepan and place the saucepan over medium heat. Cook until the sauce thickens (thicken it as per your desire)
2. Transfer into an airtight container and refrigerate until use.

3. It should last for a week if refrigerated.

4. Warm it and pour over the sundae.

Hot Fudge Sundae Sauce

| Prep: 3 min | Total: 8 min | Servings: 6-8 |

Ingredients

- 1/2 cup non-dairy milk of your choice
- 2/3 cup vegan chocolate chips
- 1/2 teaspoon sea salt

Instructions

1. Add all the ingredients to a saucepan and place the saucepan over medium heat. Cook until the sauce thickens (thicken it as per your desire). Stir constantly.
2. Transfer into an airtight container and refrigerate until use.
3. It should last for a week if refrigerated.
4. Warm it and pour over the sundae.

Peanut Butter Hot Fudge

| Prep: 3 min | Total: 8 min | Servings: 10 |

Ingredients

- 2/3 cup creamy, natural butter
- 2/3 cup vegan chocolate chips
- 1 cup full fat coconut milk
- 2 tablespoons maple syrup

Instructions

1. Add all the ingredients to a saucepan and place the saucepan over medium heat. Cook until the chocolate is almost melted. Stir constantly. Remove from heat.

2. Transfer into an airtight container and refrigerate until use.

3. It should last for a week if refrigerated.

4. Warm it and pour over the sundae.

Chocolate Sauce

| Prep: 3 min | Total: 5 min | Servings: 10 |

Ingredients

- 10 tablespoons melted coconut oil
- 10 teaspoons agave syrup or sugar or sweetener of your choice
- 10 tablespoon cocoa powder, unsweetened

Instructions

1. Add all the ingredients to a bowl and whisk until well combined.

Caramel Sauce

| Prep: 3 min | Total: 5 min | Servings: 10 |

Ingredients

- 1 1/2 cups brown sugar
- 1/2 teaspoon sea salt
- 1/3 cup vegan margarine
- 3 tablespoons non-dairy milk

Instructions

1. Place a heavy bottomed pan over medium heat.
2. Add all the ingredients to the pan and bring to a boil. Stir frequently.

3. Increase the heat to medium-high for a couple of minutes until it begins to caramelize.

4. Remove from heat and cool for 15 minutes before serving

Sundae Recipes

Refer to the section on sorbets, ice creams and sauces

Create your own Sundaes

Ingredients:

- Ice creams of your choice
- Sauces of your choice
- Toppings of your choice like fruits, nuts, chocolate chips, etc.

Instructions

1. Place scoops of ice creams of your choice.
2. Add toppings of your choice.
3. Pour sauce of your choice and serve.

4. Enjoy!

Buster Parfait

| Prep: 3 min | Total: 5 min | Servings: 4 |

Ingredients

- 4 scoops soft serve ice cream
- 4 tablespoons peanut butter hot fudge sauce or more if desired
- 1/2 cup peanuts, roasted, roughly chopped

Instructions

1. Scoop ice cream into 4 bowls
2. Drizzle sauce over it.
3. Sprinkle peanuts and serve.
4. Enjoy!

Banana Ice Cream Sundae

| Prep: 3 min | Total: 5 min | Servings: 4 |

Ingredients

- 4 scoops vegan banana ice cream
- 4 tablespoons vegan chocolate sauce
- Toppings of your choice

Instructions

1. Scoop ice cream into 4 bowls
2. Drizzle sauce over it.
3. Sprinkle toppings and serve.
4. Enjoy!

Grilled Banana Split

| Prep: 3 min | Total: 5 min | Servings: 6 |

Ingredients

- 6 scoops vegan coconut ice cream
- 6 bananas, halved lengthwise
- 6 tablespoons chocolate sauce
- 1/3 cup walnuts, chopped

Instructions

1. Place a stovetop grill plate over medium heat and preheat it or use a nonstick pan with a little coconut oil.

2. Place bananas over it and grill for 2-3 minutes per side until golden brown.
3. Take 6 serving plates. Place 2 banana halves over each of the plates.
4. Place one scoop ice cream over the bananas.
5. Drizzle chocolate sauce over it and serve.

Dairy Free Yogurt Sundae with Fruit & Chocolate Sauce

| Prep: 5 min | Total: 10 min | Servings: 2 |

Ingredients

- 1/2 cup frozen berries
- 1/4 cup vegan chocolate chips
- 2 tablespoons white sugar
- 2 (8-ounce) containers vanilla soy yogurt
- 6 tablespoons soy creamer or soy milk
- 2 tablespoons chopped nuts

Instructions

1. Place the frozen berries into a microwave proof bowl. Sprinkle the sugar over the berries and mix well. Place the bowl into the microwave and cook on the high setting for about 40 seconds.
2. In another larger microwave safe bowl, place the margarine and chocolate chips together. Place in the microwave and cook for about 45 seconds at 60% power or until melted.
3. Whisk well using a fork and slowly trickle the soy creamer or soy milk in and mix with the fork until well combined.
4. Using a round spoon, place a quenelle of the vanilla soy yogurt in a mixing bowl. Spoon a little-cooked fruit over the soy yogurt quenelle. Pour a spoon of the prepared chocolate sauce over it and sprinkle the nuts over it.
5. Repeat with rest of the yogurt, fruit and chocolate sauce.
6. Serve immediately.
7. Enjoy!

Chocolate Sundae

| Prep: 15 min | Total: 10 min | Servings: 4 |

Ingredients

- 4 scoops vegan chocolate ice cream
- 1 banana, peeled, sliced
- 4 tablespoons walnuts, chopped, toasted
- 1 cup strawberries, halved
- Chocolate sauce as desired
- A few cacao nibs
- 4 sprigs mint

Instructions

1. Take 4 sundae glasses. Place a layer of half the strawberries followed by banana.
2. Place a scoop of chocolate ice cream.
3. Layer again with strawberries and banana.
4. Sprinkle walnuts and cacao nibs.
5. Drizzle chocolate sauce and serve.

Triple Sundae

Prep: 15 min	Total: 10 min	Servings: 6

Ingredients

- 1 cup heavy cream
- 6 scoops vegan chocolate ice cream
- 6 scoops vegan vanilla ice cream
- 6 scoops vegan raspberry sorbet
- 1/2 cup fresh strawberries, halved to garnish
- Warm berry sauce as required

Instructions

1. Add about a tablespoon each of warm berry sauce into tall sundae glasses.
2. Place a scoop of vanilla ice cream in each glass.
3. Drizzle a tablespoon each of warm berry sauce over it.
4. Place a scoop of chocolate ice cream in each glass.
5. Drizzle a tablespoon each of warm berry sauce over it.
6. Place a scoop of raspberry sorbet in each glass.
7. Place a blob of cream over sorbet.
8. Garnish with strawberries and serve immediately.

Conclusion

I would like to thank you once again for downloading this book!

To conclude, the vegan diet is not the boring and tasteless diet it is usually considered to be. With a little modification, almost all the recipes in the world can be made vegan-friendly. This book shows you that how you can prepare a variety of delicious ice creams, sundaes and sorbets without adding any unhealthy dairy products.

All the recipes in this book use ingredients that are easily available in any vegan household. So, if you have midnight cravings or need to whip something up quickly, you don't need to rush to your nearest supermarket!

I would like to take the opportunity to once again thank you for purchasing this book and I hope that you found the content of this book helpful!

Stay safe; stay healthy and enjoy these ice creams!

101 Chocolate Vegan Recipes

A Vegan Cookbook Delight!

About the author

Sam Kuma is passionate about sharing his culinary experience to the world. His work involves modernization of healthy diet plans. He has written/published books for vegan food, ketogenic food, paleo food, dash food and several foods from other ethnic cuisines. His main focus is to make healthy diets like vegan and ketogenic mainstream by producing delicious, appetizing recipes. In his first two books regarding Vegan recipes, he has produced delicious Vegan Chocolate meals, Vegan Desserts, Vegan Ice Creams, Vegan Burgers and Sandwiches. Below is a link to his other cookbooks:

Sam's Cookbooks

Disclaimer

Copyright © 2016

All Rights Reserved.

No part of this eBook can be transmitted or reproduced in any form including print, electronic, photocopying, scanning, mechanical or recording without prior written permission from the author.

While the author has taken utmost efforts to ensure the accuracy of the written content, all readers are advised to follow information mentioned herein at their own risk. The author cannot be held responsible for any personal or commercial damage caused by information. All readers are encouraged to seek professional advice when needed.

Introduction

Chocolate anyone?

There are very few people who would say 'no' to that. Chocolate is heaven in your mouth. Chocolate is the one reason to live. Chocolate is better than, ahem, anything!

It's not just a bittersweet piece of dark brown goodness, oh no, chocolate has so much more significance. It is considered to be the epitome of a romantic gift. It is the best mood booster. It's everyone's favourite comfort food.

So when you make the transition to a vegan lifestyle, why should you abandon a vital lifeline like chocolate?

The thought of abandoning chocolate for life is enough to deter people from their chosen vegan lifestyle. However, don't let this scary thought sway your decision.

Going vegan is the best choice that you can make for yourself and the environment.

Do you have pets? Did you have a childhood pet?
If you answered yes then you'll know that animals are much more than just meat, fur and leather. They're living creatures with very different and colourful personalities. No two animals (or birds) are alike. They have their own wants, needs, preferences and dreams. Thinking that we

(humans) are above them or that they are just food is wrong on so many levels.

Every year, so many cows, chickens, goats and lambs do not even get a chance to live out their life. They are kept in close quarters where they live in their own filth and barely get a chance experience any good in life. As soon as they grow up, they are paraded towards their death so that people like you and me can have their steaks and chicken roast.

Even the so-called 'organic' and 'free-range' animal products are nothing but a scam. Those animals often live in just as deplorable conditions as their other counterparts. Labeling on the package doesn't change their situation.

These animals deserve a chance to live and flourish.

In addition to the ethical plight, veganism also has many health advantages. Many of us now suffer from problems like hypertension, cardiac issues, cholesterol, obesity and high uric acid. High consumption of animal products is a significant contributor to these.

Plant-derived food is cholesterol free, fat-free and healthier. Decide for yourself which is better; some baked snow peas or a round steak? Both have a good protein content but peas are much safer and healthier.

Then there's also our environment that we have to account for. Animal farming is the leading contributor to the production of greenhouse gases. Simple agriculture farming is much better for the health of our earth. We should all be just as concerned about the health of our planet as we are about our own health.

Either way, veganism is the answer. It is not a restrictive diet by any means. Once you turn your focus away from animal products, you'll be surprised to learn how many delicious vegan options are out there.

Then there's also chocolate. However, sadly, many commercial chocolate options come accompanied with milk, butter and other dairy products. This makes them a no-go for vegans.

With this problem in mind, I decided to compile this book. Here you'll find 101 delicious chocolate recipes. All of these recipes are vegan and very different from one another, so you'll have something for every occasion and mood.

All the recipes included have also a subsection containing all the nutritional information for my weight watcher friends out there. All the nutritional information given is per serving.

No matter what your preferences are, I am confident that this book will have you covered.

So let's dive into a world of chocolaty goodness!

Breakfast

1. Chocolate Chia Smoothie Pudding

A smoothie pudding? What's that? You might ask. Well it's a new hybrid drink that is a cross between a smoothie and a pudding. It's a fluffy, thick smoothie, like an ice-cream shake, but in a fun chocolate flavour.

Serves 2

<u>Ingredients</u>

1 Cup Almond Milk

1/4 Cup Chia Seeds

3 Tablespoons Cocoa Powder

1/2 Teaspoon Vanilla Extract

6 Pitted Dates

A Pinch of Sea Salt

Procedure

1. Pour about 1/2 cup milk into an ice-tray. You would need about 4-5 almond milk ice cubes.

2. Place the ice tray in the freezer and freeze overnight.

3. The next morning, add the remaining almond milk to a blender.

4. Add in cocoa powder, vanilla extract, dates, chia seeds and salt to the blender as well.

5. Blend on high speed until everything is homogenous.

6. Add the almond milk ice cubes to two glasses.

7. Pour the smoothie over them.

8. Enjoy immediately.

Nutritional Information

Calories: 245

Carbohydrates: 19.9 g

Proteins: 3.2 g

Fats: 17.3 g

2. Thin Chocolate Crepes

Serves 6

Ingredients

1 Cup Flour

1/2 Cup Water

1/2 Cup Almond Milk

1/4 Cup Cocoa Powder

1/4 Cup Maple Syrup

1/2 Teaspoon Baking Powder

Oil for frying

Fillings and toppings of choice

Procedure

1. Mix all the ingredients together except for the coconut oil.

2. The mixture should be thin and watery.

3. Place in the refrigerator for about an hour. This step is necessary.

4. When ready to cook, take the batter out of the fridge.

5. Heat a little coconut oil in a frying pan.

6. Ladle about 1/4 cup of the batter into the pan. Tilt the pan sideways to ensure that the entire surface is covered.

7. Cook for about two minutes or until the sides begin to brown.

8. Flip and cook for another two minutes.

9. Once it's cooked, move it onto a plate. Continue this process till all the batter is completely used up.

10. Serve with fillings and toppings of choice.

Nutritional Information

Calories: 164

Carbohydrates: 28 g

Proteins: 3.3 g

Fats: 5.5 g

3. Chocolate Hazelnut Spread

My favorite breakfast is chocolate hazelnut spread on toast. Unfortunately, the store bought version is neither vegan nor healthy. So here is a recipe which you can duplicate at home.

Yields 2 Mason Jars

Ingredients

2 Cups Roasted Hazelnuts

1/2 Cup Almond Milk

1/4 Cup Maple Syrup

1/4 Cup Cocoa Powder

2 Teaspoons Oil

1/4 Teaspoons Salt

Procedure

1. Add roasted hazelnuts to a food processor and blend. First, they will turn to powder. Keep blending and eventually it will turn to butter.

2. Add in the rest of the ingredients and continue to blend until a smooth, creamy consistency is achieved.

3. Transfer to a mason jar and store in the refrigerator.

Nutritional Information

Calories: 41

Carbohydrates: 4.7 g

Proteins: 0.4 g

Fats: 2.7 g

4. Double Chocolate Oatmeal

A warm, cosy bowl of oatmeal is a perfect start to just about any day. And it's even better with chocolate.

Serves 2

Ingredients

4 Cups Water

1 Cup Rolled Oats

1/2 Cup Almond Milk

1/2 Cup Grated Chocolate

1 Tablespoon Cocoa Powder

1 Teaspoon Vanilla Extract

Brown Sugar to Taste

Procedure

1. Soak rolled oats in water and bring to a boil. Slow cook until done.

2. Melt the chocolate over a double boiler and add in the milk, cocoa powder, vanilla extract and brown sugar. Mix well.

3. The oats should not be too watery.

4. Mix the chocolate and oats together. Then top the oats with chopped nuts, chocolate chips or fruit.

5. Enjoy!

Nutritional Information

Calories: 531

Carbohydrates: 57.9 g

Proteins: 10.5 g

Fats: 29.8 g

5. Brownie Breakfast Bake

Do you like the floury taste of cake batter? Well I secretly do... I find excuses to taste it while I am baking. If you are like me, then here is a recipe that recreates that taste.

Serves 1

Ingredients

1/3 Cup Rolled Oats

1/3 Cup Almond Milk

2 Tablespoon Flour

2 Tablespoon Chocolate Chips

1 Tablespoon Cocoa Powder

1 Tablespoon Maple Syrup

1 Teaspoon Coconut Oil

1/2 Teaspoon Vanilla Extract

1/4 Teaspoon Baking Powder

Procedure

1. Mix together all the dry ingredients in a large bowl.

2. In another bowl, mix together all the wet ingredients.

3. Make a well in the middle of the dry ingredients and pour in the wet ingredients. Mix to form a batter.

4. Add the chocolate chips.

5. Pour into a pre-greased oven-friendly bowl.

6. Bake for 12 minutes at 325 degrees.

7. Enjoy!

Nutritional Information

Calories: 567

Carbohydrates: 64.5 g

Proteins: 9.6 g

Fats: 32.5 g

6. Vegan Chocolate Waffles

Being vegan does not mean that you have to miss out on the classic waffle breakfast. Waffles are easily reproduced without any milk or eggs. You just have to cook a little bit longer as egg free waffles take a little more time to set.

Serves 5-6

Ingredients

1 Cup Flour

1 Cup Almond Milk

1/4 Cup Agave Syrup

4 Tablespoons Cocoa Powder

3 Tablespoons Dark Chocolate Chips

2 Tablespoons Vegan Butter

1/2 Teaspoon Baking Powder

1/2 Teaspoon Vanilla Extract

A Pinch of Ground Cinnamon

A Pinch of Salt

Procedure

1. Mix together all the ingredients in a bowl to make a batter.

2. Make sure that there are no lumps.

3. Ladle some of the mixture onto the waffle iron

4. Cook according to your preferred setting but a little longer than usual.

5. Plate and top with vegan ice-cream of choice.

6. Enjoy!

Nutritional Information

Calories: 237

Carbohydrates: 33.9 g

Proteins: 4 g

Fats: 11.2 g

7. Banana-Chocolate Chip Waffles

The combination of bananas and chocolate never gets old. So here is a recipe for waffles in this combination. Pair it with some vegan banana ice cream and this recipe will brighten your mornings.

Serves 5

Ingredients

1 Cup Flour

1 Cup Soy Milk

1/4 Cup Semi-Sweet Chocolate Chips

1/4 Cup Rolled Oats

2 1/2 Teaspoons Baking Powder

1/4 Teaspoon Salt

2 Bananas

1 Flax Egg

Procedure

1. Mix together all the ingredients in a large bowl until smooth batter forms.

2. Ladle into a waffle iron and cook like normal. Just give it a little more time to set.

3. Plate and drizzle generously with maple syrup.

4. Pair with vegan banana ice cream and you are good to go.

Nutritional Information

Calories: 239

Carbohydrates: 44 g

Proteins: 3.5 g

Fats: 3.5 g

8. Chai Chocolate Oatmeal

Traditional chai tea in India has an amazing characteristic. If you are a chai lover, then you will really like this translation of flavour into a bowl of oatmeal.

Serves 2

Ingredients

3/4 Cup Water

3/4 Cup Cashew Milk

1/2 Cup Hot Cereal

2 Tablespoons Cocoa Powder

1 Tablespoon Maple Syrup

1/2 Teaspoon Ground Cinnamon

1/4 Teaspoon Ground Ginger

1/4 Teaspoon Sea Salt

1/8 Teaspoon Ground Cloves

1/8 Teaspoon Ground Cardamom

1 Black Tea Bag

Procedure

1. Add milk and water to a boil and add in all the spices. Lower the heat and allow to simmer for about 5 minutes or until the mixture becomes fragrant.

2. Add in the cereal and cook according to package instructions.

3. Add in a tea bag and swirl around about 10 times and then discard.

4. Add in the cocoa powder and stir.

5. Pour into a bowl and enjoy.

Nutritional Information

Calories: 41

Carbohydrates: 10.5 g

Proteins: 1 g

Fats: 0.8 g

9. Banana and Chocolate Porridge

As delicious as Goldilocks' Three Bears Porridge

Serves 1

Ingredients

1/2 Cup Water

1/2 Cup Almond Milk

1/2 Rolled Oats

1 Teaspoon Cocoa Powder

1/2 Teaspoon Vanilla Extract

1 Banana

Procedure

1. Bring almond milk and water to a boil.

2. Add in oats and allow to simmer until the mixture begins to thicken.

3. Add in the cocoa powder and vanilla extract. Stir.

4. Pour into a bowl and slice banana on top.

5. Serve.

Nutritional Information

Calories: 391

Carbohydrates: 34.9 g

Proteins: 4.4 g

Fats: 29.2 g

10. Chocolate Tapioca Pudding

A smooth, creamy breakfast treat.

Serves 2

Ingredients

1 Can Coconut Milk

2 Cups Soy Milk

1/3 Cup Small Tapioca Balls

1/3 Cup Maple Syrup

1/2 Cup Chocolate Chips

1 Teaspoon Vanilla Extract

1/4 Teaspoon Salt

Procedure

1. Soak the tapioca in soy milk overnight.

2. In the morning, combine with coconut milk, vanilla extract and maple syrup.

3. Heat the mixture but do not bring to a boil. Keep stirring until the mixture begins to thicken.

4. Pour into a bowl and add the chocolate chips.

5. The tapioca balls should be suspended in the pudding and not sink to the bottom.

6. Enjoy while still warm.

Nutritional Information

Calories: 500

Carbohydrates: 75.8 g

Proteins: 11.2 g

Fats: 16.9 g

11. Chocolate French Toast

French toast is the epitome of recycling and reusing. You don't need any fancy ingredients or even new ingredients. Just explore your pantry and fridge and you'll already have all the ingredients you need. Perfect for busy mornings.

Serves 2

Ingredients

4 Pieces Stale French Bread

4 Flax Eggs

1/3 Cup Powdered Sugar

1/2 Cup Almond Milk

1 Tablespoon Granulated Sugar

1 Tablespoon Vegan Butter

1 Tablespoon Cocoa Powder

1/2 Teaspoon Vanilla Extract

Oil

Procedure

1. Whisk together milk, powdered sugar and flax eggs.

2. In another bowl, beat vegan butter with granulated sugar until it is dissolved.

3. Combine the two and stir in cocoa powder and vanilla extract.

4. Heat oil in a pan.

5. Dip the pieces of bread into the mixture until it soaks up some of the mixture.

6. Fry until golden brown on both sides.

7. Drizzle with some maple or chocolate syrup and serve.

Nutritional Information

Calories: 449

Carbohydrates: 74.4 g

Proteins: 8.6 g

Fats: 14.7 g

12. Chocolate Chip and Pumpkin Pancakes

Pancakes drizzled with maple syrup…....Mmmm……

This sounds like heaven. This is a delicious way to use the fall staple pumpkin puree. Chocolate and pumpkin complement each other perfectly and combining them in pancakes is just...genius!

Serves 4

<u>Ingredients</u>

1 1/2 Cups All Purpose Flour

1 1/2 Cup Soy Milk

3/4 Cups Chocolate Chips

3 Tablespoons Pumpkin Puree

3 Tablespoons Sugar

3 Tablespoons Canola Oil

1 1/2 Tablespoons Baking Powder

1 3/4 Teaspoons Ground Cinnamon

1/2 Teaspoon Grated Ginger

1/3 Teaspoon Ground Nutmeg

A Pinch of Salt

Oil for Frying

Procedure

1. Mix together all the dry ingredients.

2. In another bowl, mix together all the wet ingredients.

3. Make a well in the middle of the dry ingredients and pour in the wet ingredients.

4. Mix in the chocolate chips.

5. Heat some oil in a pan and ladle about 1/4 cup of mixture.

6. Cook until bubbles pop on the surface.

7. Flip and cook until done.

8. Serve with toppings of choice.

Nutritional Information

Calories: 529

Carbohydrates: 73.9 g

Proteins: 22.1 g

Fats: 10.5 g

Bakes and Cakes

13. Chocolate Mug Cake

This recipe might come off as one of those gimmicky recipes that say that they only need 1 minute but actually end up taking an hour. It might be hard to believe but this cake actually does take only a minute to make.

Don't believe me? Try it out for yourself.

It is the perfect midnight snack as it is so simple and quick to make.

Serves 1

Ingredients

3 Tablespoons Spelt Flour

3 Tablespoons Cocoa Powder

3 Tablespoons Almond Milk

3 Tablespoons Oil

1 Tablespoons Sugar

1/2 Teaspoon Vanilla Extract

A Pinch of Salt

Procedure

1. Combine together all the dry ingredients in a large coffee mug.

2. Add in the wet ingredients and mix well.

3. Remove the spoon and microwave for a minute.

4. Remove from the oven, allow to cool a little and then eat straight from the mug.

5. Have fun!

Nutritional Information

Calories: 205

Carbohydrates: 30 g

Proteins: 5.5 g

Fats: 12 g

14. Oatmeal and Chocolate Pie

Oatmeal is a common breakfast across the world. It is very customizable and usually has a bland taste. That is what makes it so versatile as well as this recipe proves. Like in this pie, it is used as a base. This makes this recipe high in fiber, great for health and absolutely delicious.

Serves 8

Ingredients

3/4 Cup Steel Cut Oats

3/4 Cup Pancake Syrup

1/2 Cup Almond Milk

1/2 Cup Coconut Oil

1/2 Cup Chocolate Chips

1/2 Cup Chopped Walnuts

2 Flax Eggs

Procedure

1. Mix together all the ingredients in a large bowl.

2. Line a pie shell with parchment paper and pour the batter into it.

3. Bake for 1 hour at 350 degrees.

4. Cool and slice.

5. Enjoy!

Nutritional Information

Calories: 354

Carbohydrates: 31.1 g

Proteins: 4 g

Fats: 25.4 g

15. Pumpkin Chocolate Loaf

If one of these is lying around in the fridge, it is so hard to resist. Often, I will bake this loaf and store the leftover in the refrigerator. Then whenever I open the fridge, I am tempted to gobble it all down simply because it is so good!

Serves 5-6

Ingredients

1 1/2 Cups Flour

1 Cup Diced Pumpkin

1 Cup Brown Sugar

1/2 Cup Coconut Milk

4 Tablespoons Cocoa Powder

2 Tablespoons Coconut Oil

1 Tablespoon Molasses

1 Teaspoons Instant Coffee

1 Teaspoon Baking Powder

3/4 Teaspoon Ground Cinnamon

1/2 Teaspoon Baking Powder

1/2 Teaspoon Salt

1 Large Apple

Procedure

1. Peel, core and dice the apple.
2. Add the cubed apples, pumpkin and coconut milk in a food processor. Blend until smooth puree forms.
3. Add in the coconut oil and blend once again.
4. In a large bowl, sift together all the dry ingredients.
5. Make a well in the middle of the dry ingredients and pour in the wet ingredients.
6. Mix well to make a smooth batter.
7. Pour into a bread loaf and bake for 20 minutes at 400 degrees.

8. Then lower the temperature to 350 degrees and bake for 30 minutes.

9. Cool on a wire rack before slicing.

10. Enjoy!

Nutritional Information

Calories: 343

Carbohydrates: 62.4 g

Proteins: 4.9 g

Fats: 10.3 g

16. Chocolate Chip Bagels

Bagels for breakfasts. Nothing can get better than that.

Serves 3-4

Ingredients

3 1/4 Cups Flour

1 3/4 Cup Almond Milk

1 Cup Dark Chocolate Chips

2 Tablespoons Oil

3 Teaspoons Guar Gum

2 1/2 Teaspoons Yeast

1 Teaspoon Vanilla Extract

3/4 Teaspoon Salt

Procedure

1. Heat about 1/2 cup water in a saucepan. Do not bring to boil. Remove from heat just before bubbles begin to appear.

2. Add the hot water to yeast and set aside.

3. In a separate bowl, combine together flour, chocolate chips, guar gum and salt.

4. In another bowl, mix together almond milk, vanilla extract and oil.

5. Add the watery mixture to the dry mixture slowly and knead to form a dough.

6. Take about golf ball sized dough and roll elongated.

7. Then meet the two ends to form the shape of a bagel.

8. Line on a baking tray.

9. Cover with a cloth and allow to sit for about half an hour so that the bagel rises.

10. Wrap each bagel with parchment paper.

11. Bring water to a roaring boil and drop a bagel into it. Remove after 30 seconds and place on the baking sheet again.

12. Bake for 15 minutes at 450 degrees.

13. Enjoy!

<u>Nutritional Information</u>

Calories: 422

Carbohydrates: 52.2 g

Proteins: 7.3 g

Fats: 20.4 g

17. Chocolate Banana Bread

Do you have some over-ripened bananas in your fridge? If yes, then perfect! This recipe doesn't call for any special ingredients and can be made quite easily. You don't have to look beyond your pantry. Just make sure you have some over-ripened bananas in hand.

Serves 4-5

Ingredients

1 1/2 Cups Flour

1 Cup Chocolate Chips

1 Cup Almond Milk

3/4 Cup Brown Sugar

1/3 Cup Olive Oil

1/4 Cup Cocoa Powder

1 Teaspoon Vanilla Extract

1 Teaspoon Baking Powder

1/2 Teaspoon Baking Soda

1/2 Teaspoon Salt

3 Over Ripe Bananas

Procedure

1. Sift together flour, sugar, cocoa powder, baking powder, baking soda and salt.

2. In a bowl, mash the bananas until smooth.

3. Add milk, oil and vanilla extract to the mashed bananas.

4. Make a well in the middle of the dry ingredients and pour in the wet ingredients.

5. Mix well to form a batter.

6. Pour into a pre-greased bread pan.

7. Bake for 45 minutes at 375 degrees.

8. Cool and then slice.

Nutritional Information

Calories: 637

Carbohydrates: 75.5 g

Proteins: 8.3 g

Fats: 35.8 g

18. Chickpea Blondies

I like the recipes that require very little dishwashing. Nobody likes a hoard of dishes after you've finished eating. That is one reason I love this recipe. The other reason being that these are incredibly delicious.

Serves 9

Ingredients

2 Cups Boiled and Drained Chickpeas

3/4 Cup Maple Syrup

1/2 Cup Grated Dark Chocolate

1/2 Cup Chunky Peanut Butter

1 1/2 Teaspoons Vanilla Extract

1 Teaspoon Baking Powder

1/2 Teaspoon Salt

Procedure

1. Add all the ingredients to a food processor.

2. Blend on high for 3-5 minutes. Scrape off the sides periodically.

3. Line an 8x8 inch pan with parchment paper.

4. Pour in the mixture.

5. Bake for 50 minutes at 375 degrees.

6. Cool, cut into squares and enjoy!

Nutritional Information

Calories: 367

Carbohydrates: 53.5 g

Proteins: 12.7 g

Fats: 12.7 g

19. Chocolate Chip Muffins

Muffins come in so many shapes, sizes and colours. However, they are all delightful. From fun fruity ones to chocolate chips ones, all are awesome! This is a simple recipe that recreates the classic chocolate chip muffins in a vegan-friendly way.

Serves 12

Ingredients

2 1/2 Cups Wheat Flour

1/2 Cup Chocolate Chips

1/2 Cup Coconut Palm Sugar

1/2 Cup Almond Milk

1/4 Cup Olive Oil

1 1/2 Teaspoons Baking Powder

1 Teaspoon Vanilla Extract

4 Bananas

Procedure

1. Blend together almond milk, vanilla extract and bananas in a blender.
2. In a bowl, sift together flour, sugar and baking powder.
3. Mix the almond milkshake into the flour mixture and stir to make a batter. Use a whisk to ensure that there are no lumps.
4. Add in the chocolate chips and gently stir again.
5. Grease a muffin tray.
6. Use an ice-cream scoop to scoop batter into the cups.
7. Bake for 25 minutes at 350 degrees or until a toothpick inserted in the middle comes out clean.
8. Cool on a wire rack and then serve.

Nutritional Information

Calories: 228

Carbohydrates: 33.9 g

Proteins: 3.9 g

Fats: 9.1 g

20. Chocolate Chip Biscotti

A fancy looking tea time treat for all my chocolate chips lovers out there.

Serves 7-8

Ingredients

3 Cups Cashew Meal

1/3 Cup Chocolate Chips

1/4 Cup Maple Syrup

1 Tablespoon Tapioca Starch

1/2 Teaspoon Baking Soda

A Pinch of Salt

1 Flax Egg

Procedure

1. Combine together all the dry ingredients in a large bowl.

2. Whisk together the flax egg and maple syrup.

3. Pour the flax egg mixture over the dry ingredients and begin to mix to form a dough. Use some warm water if needed.

4. Use your hands to knead the dough. Then take small pieces and make them into long shapes. Place on parchment paper.

5. Bake for 22 minutes at 350 degrees.

6. Then turn the sides and bake for another 12 minutes.

7. Allow to cool before serving.

Nutritional Information

Calories: 127

Carbohydrates: 14.8 g

Proteins: 2.4 g

Fats: 6.6 g

21. Protein Donuts

Donuts are notorious for being extremely unhealthy. Well not these ones. In fact, these are much healthier than a regular deep fried option.

Serves 3

Ingredients

2 Tablespoons Coconut Flour

2 Tablespoons Non-Dairy Milk

1 Tablespoon Peanut Butter

1 Flax Egg

1/2 Banana

Procedure

1. Combine together all the ingredients and mix well.
2. Line donut pans with some parchment paper.

3. Pour in the mixture.

4. Bake for 10 minutes at 350 degrees.

5. Allow to cool a little before popping out.

6. Drizzle with a chocolate <u>sauce or glaze</u> of choice.

<u>Nutritional Information</u>

Calories: 95

Carbohydrates: 9.1 g

Proteins: 2.8 g

Fats: 6 g

22. Three Ingredient Brownies

This is to satisfy your occasional brownie craving.

Serves 3

Ingredients

1/2 Cup Almond Butter

1/4 Cup Cocoa Powder

3 Medium Bananas

Procedure

1. Add all the ingredients to a food processor and blend until smooth.

2. Pour into a pre-greased baking pan.

3. Bake for 20 minutes at 325 degrees.

4. Slice and serve.

Nutritional Information

Calories: 386

Carbohydrates: 38.2 g

Proteins: 11.4 g

Fats: 24.9 g

23. Chocolate Orange Scones

Tea anyone?

Tea and scones. Very British. Very Proper.

Serves 15

Ingredients

2 Cups Flour

3/4 Cups Coconut Cream

1/2 Cup Chocolate Chips

6 Tablespoons Vegan Butter

1 Tablespoon Baking Powder

1 Teaspoon Orange Zest

1/2 Teaspoon Vanilla Extract

A Pinch of Salt

Procedure

1. Add all the ingredients apart from chocolate chips to a food processor and pulse to make a dough.

2. Pour into a bowl and fold in the chocolate chips.

3. Dust the kitchen counters with some flour and knead the dough using your hands.

4. Make into a square and cut into small squares and then cut them diagonally to form triangles.

5. Place on a baking tray and bake for 12 minutes at 400 degrees.

6. Cool and enjoy.

Nutritional Information

Calories: 120

Carbohydrates: 17.2 g

Proteins: 2.4 g

Fats: 4.7 g

24. Chocolate Chip Scones

Another version for those of you who are not a fan of the zesty orange flavour. These are double chocolate and taste amazing!

Serves 15

<u>Ingredients</u>

2 Cups Flour

3/4 Cups Soy Cream

1/2 Cup Chocolate Chips

1/2 Cup Dark Cocoa Powder

6 Tablespoons Margarine

1 Tablespoon Baking Powder

1/2 Teaspoon Vanilla Extract

A Pinch of Salt

Procedure

1. Add all the ingredients apart from chocolate chips to a food processor and pulse to make a dough.
2. Pour into a bowl and fold in the chocolate chips.
3. Dust the kitchen counters with some flour and knead the dough using your hands.
4. Make into a square and cut into small squares and then cut them diagonally to form triangles.
5. Place on a baking tray and bake for 12 minutes at 400 degrees.
6. Cool and enjoy.

Nutritional Information

Calories: 127

Carbohydrates: 1812 g

Proteins: 2.6 g

Fats: 4.9 g

25. Dark Chocolate Zucchini Cake

This is a great way to sneak some vegetables into your diet without it being too apparent. This cake is deliciously moist and chewy. You can store it for up to a week and use it as for breakfast or as a dessert.

Serves 6-8

Ingredients

2 Cups Grated Zucchini

1 1/2 Cups Flour

1 Cup Semi-Sweet Chocolate Chips

1/3 Cup Cocoa Powder

1/3 Cup Canola Oil

1/2 Cup Granulated Sugar

1/2 Cup Brown Sugar

1/2 Teaspoon Vanilla Extract

1/2 Teaspoon Salt

1/2 Teaspoon Baking Soda

1/4 Teaspoon Baking Powder

2 Flax Eggs

Procedure

1. Sift all the dry ingredients together.

2. In another bowl, mix together all the wet ingredients.

3. Make a well in the middle of the dry ingredients and pour in the wet mixture.

4. Stir to form a batter.

5. Fold in grated zucchini and chocolate chips.

6. Pour into a pre-greased cake pan.

7. Bake for 50 minutes at 350 degrees.

8. Cool, slice and serve.

Nutritional Information

Calories: 300

Carbohydrates: 47.3 g

Proteins: 3.9 g

Fats: 11.8 g

26. Coffee and Chocolate Muffins

Ultra-rich and spongy. These are filled with tiny chocolate chunks so that each bite is a delight.

Hey! That rhymed!

Serves 12

Ingredients

2 Cups Flour

1 Cup Espresso

1/3 Cup Cocoa Powder

1/3 Cup Brown Sugar

1/3 Cup Chopped Dark Chocolate

1/2 Cup Granulated Sugar

1/4 Cup Soy Yogurt

1 Tablespoon Instant Coffee

1 Tablespoon Baking Powder

1 Teaspoon Vanilla Extract

1/2 Teaspoon Ground Cinnamon

1/2 Teaspoon Sea Salt

1 Flax Egg

Procedure

1. Sift all the dry ingredients together.

2. In another bowl, mix all the wet ingredients together.

3. Mix the two together to form a batter.

4. Fold in the chocolate chips.

5. Grease a muffin tray.

6. Fill each muffin cup with 2/3rds of with batter.

7. Bake at 375 degrees for 20 minutes.

8. Cool on a wire rack before serving.

Nutritional Information

Calories: 160

Carbohydrates: 33.5 g

Proteins: 3.2 g

Fats: 2 g

27. Avocado Chocolate Cake

Avocado lends this cake a smooth, creamy texture but you won't be able to taste it at all.

Serves 8

Ingredients

1 Cup Pastry Flour

3/4 Cup Granulated Sugar

3/4 Cup Water

1/2 Cup Semi-Sweet Chocolate Chips

1/4 Cup Avocado Puree

1/4 Cup Soy Yogurt

6 Tablespoons Cocoa Powder

2 Teaspoons Vanilla Extract

1/2 Teaspoon Baking Soda

A Pinch of Salt

Procedure

1. Add avocados, yogurt, water and yogurt to a food processor. Blend.

2. Slowly add flour and keep on blending until smooth paste forms.

3. Add in the rest of the ingredients and blend to form a smooth batter.

4. Grease a cake pan with some cooking oil.

5. Bake for 45-50 minutes at 350 degrees or until a toothpick inserted in the middle comes out clean.

6. Decorate with a frosting of choice after cooling.

7. Slice and serve.

Nutritional Information

Calories: 130

Carbohydrates: 30.5 g

Proteins: 2.5 g

Fats: 0.9 g

28. Chocolate Filled Puff Pastry

Crispy on the outside, soft and gooey on the inside. That's the perfect puff pastry for you.

Serves 6

Ingredients

1 Puff Pastry Sheet

1/2 Cup Semi-Sweet Chocolate Chips

1/2 Cup Chopped Pecans or Walnuts

1 Tablespoon Vegan Butter

Powdered Sugar

Procedure

1. Defrost a pastry sheet and lay out about a twelve-inch sheet.
2. Melt together butter and chocolate chips over a double boiler.
3. Spread this mixture on the puff pastry sheet.
4. Sprinkle chopped pecans on top.
5. Begin to roll it up like a burrito.

6. Tuck in the end.

7. Diagonally cut into about six pieces.

8. Bake for 30 minutes at 375 degrees.

9. Cool and serve.

Nutritional Information

Calories: 64

Carbohydrates: 1 g

Proteins: 2.5 g

Fats: 6.2 g

29. Chocolate Lava Cake

This cake has borderline legendary status and very few people can get it right. It takes a bit of practice but you can get it right if you follow this recipe and hone your skills.

Serves 2

Ingredients

1/4 Cup Flour

1/4 Cup Almond Milk

1/4 Cup Apple Sauce

2 1/2 Tablespoons Sugar

2 Tablespoons Cocoa Powder

2 Tablespoons Semi-Sweet Chocolate Chips

1 Tablespoon Coconut Oil

1/2 Teaspoon Lemon Juice

1/4 Teaspoon Vanilla Extract

1/4 Teaspoon Baking Powder

Dark Chocolate

A Pinch of Salt

Procedure

1. Combine together almond milk and lemon juice. Wait for it to curdle.

2. Add in all the wet ingredients to the almond milk.

3. Then slowly, add in the dry ingredients one by one and mix to make a homogenous mixture. There should be no lumps.

4. Pour the mixture into two muffin cups.

5. Push a piece of dark chocolate into the middle of both the muffin cups and cover with the batter.

6. Bake for 15 minutes at 375 degrees or until the edges leave the pan. Do not overcook.

7. Cool for a few minutes before removing.

8. Plate and serve with vegan ice-cream of choice.

Nutritional Information

Calories: 261

Carbohydrates: 33.5 g

Proteins: 3.3 g

Fats: 14.8 g

30. Chocolate Oreo Cheesecake

This recipe yields a delicious, sweet and crunchy cake that is perfect for any occasion.

Serves 8

<u>Ingredients</u>

1 1/2 Cups Crushed <u>Vegan Oreos</u>

1/4 Cup Vegan Butter

3/4 Cup Icing Sugar

3/4 Cup Chocolate Vegan Cream Cheese

1/2 Cup Grated Dark Chocolate

1/2 Cup Whipped Coconut Cream

1 Tablespoon Cocoa Powder

20 Vegan Oreos

<u>Procedure</u>

1. Crush the Oreos by placing them in zip lock bag and flattening with a rolling pin.

2. Combine with vegan butter and press into the bottom of a cake pan.

3. Place in the freezer.

4. While it is chilling, prepare the filling by mixing coconut cream with icing sugar.

5. When dissolved, add in cream cheese, melted dark chocolate and cocoa powder. Mix well.

8. Take the crust out of the freezer and fill the pan with filling.

9. Top with some crushed Oreos.

10. Return to the freezer and chill for about 4 hours.

11. Slice and serve.

Nutritional Information

Calories: 184

Carbohydrates: 26.1 g

Proteins: 2.4 g

Fats: 9 g

31. Chocolate Hazelnut Donuts

There's nothing better than the sweet taste of a chocolate hazelnut donut!

Serves 12

Ingredients

1 Can Kidney Beans

1 Cup Wheat Flour

1 Cup Cocoa Powder

1 Cup Almond Milk

1/2 Cup Brown Sugar

4 Tablespoons Ground Hazelnuts

1 Tablespoon Vanilla Extract

Procedure

1. Add kidney beans to a food processor and make into a paste.

2. Add the wheat flour, cocoa powder, brown sugar and ground hazelnuts to form a dry mixture.

3. Slowly add in milk to form a smooth batter.

4. Pre-grease some donut pans.

5. Pour the mixture into the donut pans and bake for 12 minutes at 350 degrees.

6. Cool and cover with icing of choice.

7. Enjoy!

Nutritional Information

Calories: 136

Carbohydrates: 13.9 g

Proteins: 3.1 g

Fats: 6.8 g

32. The Depression Cake

Quite a funny name for a cake, right?

It is inspired by the depression era where resources were limited and the food was rationed so most people had to put something together using limited resources. Hence this cake was born. Simple ingredients and a simple yet delicious taste.

Serves 8

Ingredients

1 1/2 Cups Flour

1 Cup Sugar

1 Cup Water

1/3 Cup Oil

1/4 Cup Cocoa Powder

1 Teaspoon Vanilla Extract

1 Teaspoon Baking Soda

1 Teaspoon White Vinegar

For frosting:

1 Cup Sugar

1/4 Cup Cocoa Powder

2 Tablespoons Almond Butter

1 Tablespoon Almond Milk

1/4 Teaspoon Vanilla Extract

Procedure

1. Sift together all the dry ingredients for the cake.

2. Mix together all the wet ingredients for the cake.

3. Fold the wet ingredients into the dry ingredients to make a batter.

4. Pour into a baking pan and bake for 35 minutes at 350 degrees.

5. In the meanwhile, whisk together all the frosting ingredients until smooth.

6. Remove cake from oven and allow to cool.

7. Take out of the pan and spread the frosting on top. Use a wet butter knife to get a smooth finish.

8. Cut into slices and serve.

Nutritional Information

Calories: 397

Carbohydrates: 71.7 g

Proteins: 4.3 g

Fats: 12.7 g

Cookies

33. Chewy Cherry Chocolate Cookies

Chocolate Cookies are the perfect go-to snack for just about anyone. They can be eaten with milk (non-dairy) in the morning or with tea in the evening. Kids love this recipe.

Serves 9

Ingredients

2 Cups Flour

2 Cups Sugar

3/4 Cup Cocoa Powder

3/4 Cup Chocolate Chips

3/4 Cup Chopped Cherries

3/4 Cup Canola Oil

1/2 Cup Soy Milk

1 Tablespoon Flax Seeds

1 Teaspoon Vanilla Extract

1 Teaspoon Almond Extract

1 Teaspoon Baking Soda

1/4 Teaspoon Salt

Procedure

1. Add flax seeds to a food processor and blend until a powder is formed.

2. Add in the soy milk and blend again. Set aside.

3. In a large bowl, mix together all the dry ingredients.

4. Slowly add in the oil to the dry ingredients and begin to mix.

5. Add in both the extracts and the soy milk mixture.

6. Mix together to form a dough.

7. Stir in the chocolate chips and the cherries.

8. Flatten using a rolling pin and cut out small circles using a cookie

cutter.

9. Place on a baking tray lined with parchment paper.

10. Bake for 10 minutes at 350 degrees. They might seem a little wet but they are done and will be fine after cooling.

11. Store in an airtight container.

Nutritional Information

Calories: 533

Carbohydrates: 52.5 g

Proteins: 5.8 g

Fats: 4.9 g

34. Peanut Butter and Chocolate Macaroons

Macaroons are like little balls of happiness. Anyone can cheer up by just seeing them and the taste borders on being euphoric.

Serves 10

Ingredients

1 Cup Shredded Coconut

1 Cup Rolled Oats

3/4 Cup Peanut Butter (chunky or creamy, depending on your preference)

3/4 Cup Maple Syrup

1/2 Cup Chocolate Chips

1/4 Cup Cocoa Powder

1 Teaspoon Vanilla Extract

1/4 Teaspoon Salt

Procedure

1. Mix all the ingredients together in a large bowl.

2. Line a baking tray with parchment paper.

3. Take an ice-cream scoop and drop the mixture onto the parchment paper. Macaroons should be at least 1 inch apart.

4. Bake at 325 degrees for 12 minutes.

5. Allow to cool and then store in an airtight container.

6. Enjoy!

Nutritional Information

Calories: 286

Carbohydrates: 32.6 g

Proteins: 7.2 g

Fats: 15.8 g

35. Flourless Peanut Butter Biscuits

There are many reasons to avoid flour. The most obvious is a gluten allergy. The other is that flour is full of carbohydrates which you need to avoid if you are on a diet. This healthy recipe, however, is an exception to the majority of high carb desserts on the market.

Serves 7

Ingredients

15 Dark Chocolate Chunks

1 Cup Peanut Butter

1/3 Cup Flaxseeds

1/4 Cup Dates Paste (puree dates with some water)

1 Teaspoon Stevia

1 Teaspoon Vanilla Extract

Procedure

1. Heat a frying pan and toast the flax seeds until lightly brown.

2. Transfer to a food processor and blend until they are a fine powder.

3. Add in the rest of the ingredients apart from the chocolate chunks.

4. Blend until a homogenous mixture is formed.

5. Take small ball sized pieces and make them into a ball.

6. Place on a baking tray lined with parchment paper.

7. Then press down with the heel of your hand to flatten them a bit.

8. Bake for 15 minutes at 350 degrees.

9. As soon as you remove them from over, place a chocolate chunk in the middle of the cookie.

10. Return the tray to the oven for one minute.

11. Remove and allow to cool.

12. Serve.

Nutritional Information

Calories: 296

Carbohydrates: 15.3 g

Proteins: 10.9 g

Fats: 23.8 g

36. Coconut Flour Chocolate Chip Cookies

This book has so many recipes for cookies. Can you tell that I love cookies?

This recipe is perfect for those looking to avoid extra carbs and gluten-y grains. The base is made out of coconut flour which makes these melt into your mouth as you bite them. Try these out for yourself to find out.

Serves 18

Ingredients

1/4 Cup Almond Flour

1/4 Cup Coconut Flour

1/4 Cup Chocolate Chips

1/4 Cup Maple Syrup

1/2 Teaspoon Vanilla Extract

1/4 Teaspoon Baking Soda

1/4 Teaspoon Salt

Procedure

1. Mix together all the ingredients in a large bowl.

2. Allow to sit for about 15 minutes so that excess moisture is absorbed and the cookies are nice and firm.

3. In the meanwhile, line a baking tray with parchment paper.

4. Scoop small amounts of batter onto the tray and flatten to resemble the shape of a cookie.

5. Bake for 12 minutes at 350 degrees.

6. Do not touch them until they have cooled completely.

7. When at room temperature, enjoy!

Nutritional Information

Calories: 26

Carbohydrates: 4.4 g

Proteins: 0.3 g

Fats: 0.9 g

37. Chocolate Quinoa Cookies

Unbelievable! Healthy Chocolate Cookies! Rush to your kitchen now!

Serves 6

Ingredients

1/2 Cup Cooked Quinoa

1/2 Cup Quinoa Flakes

1/2 Cup Coconut Flakes

1/2 Cup Almond Butter (you can also use peanut butter)

1/3 Cup Cocoa Powder

1/4 Cup Maple Syrup

1/4 Cup Coconut Oil

A Pinch of Sea Salt

Procedure

1. Melt the coconut oil in a small saucepan

2. Add in the cocoa powder and stir until completely dissolved.

3. Add in the almond or peanut butter and stir until homogenous.

4. Remove from heat and add in the rest of the ingredients. Mix to make a gooey but crumbly mixture.

5. Line a tray with parchment paper.

6. Using a spoon, place some of the mixture onto the tray about 1 inch apart.

7. Line the entire length.

8. Place in the freezer overnight.

9. Remove and enjoy!

10. If you plan to use them over a period of time, they are best stored in the refrigerator.

Nutritional Information

Calories: 331

Carbohydrates: 25.2 g

Proteins: 7.5 g

Fats: 24.6 g

38. Dark Chocolate Shortbread Cookies

Imagine that you are sitting around lounging in your PJs and suddenly some guests show up at the door. What do you do in such a case? Well, get changed and take this shortbread dough out of your fridge to make some quick cookies. Guests entertained in literally 15 minutes.

Serves 6

Ingredients

3/4 Cup Flour

1/2 Cup Vegan Butter

1/2 Cup Dark Chocolate Chips

1/4 Cup Dark Cocoa Powder

1/4 Cup Icing Sugar

1 Teaspoon Vanilla Extract

Procedure

1. In a small bowl, mix together cocoa powder, sugar and vegan butter.

2. Add this slowly to flour and start to knead the dough.

3. When dough is ready, fold in the chocolate chips.

4. Place dough at the diagonal end of parchment paper.

5. Elongate it like a log and begin to roll. Tie in the ends like a toffee.

6. Freeze for at least 3 hours or as long as needed.

7. Place on a cutting boards and cut small disks.

8. Place the disks on a baking tray. Leave the parchment paper on.

9. Bake for 12 minutes at 350 degrees.

10. Cool before serving.

Nutritional Information

Calories: 125

Carbohydrates: 23.7 g

Proteins: 2.3 g

Fats: 2.8 g

39. Chocolate Espresso Cookies

There are endless ways to make cookies and this is another one. It is very rich, very moody and kind of bitter. If you don't like dark slightly bitter chocolate, you won't like these. Try other cookie recipes mentioned in this book. However, if you don't mind chocolate expresso cookies, then you will love these cookies!

Serves 9

Ingredients

1 1/2 Flour

1 Cup Chocolate Chips

1 Cup Vegan Butter

1/2 Cup Cocoa Powder

1/2 Cup Icing Sugar

1 Tablespoon Vanilla Extract

1 Tablespoon Espresso Powder

Procedure

1. Dissolve sugar in vegan butter. Soften it up.

2. Add in vanilla extract as well.

3. In another bowl, mix together flour, cocoa powder and espresso powder.

4. Make a batter by mixing the two. Fold in the chocolate chips.

5. Use an ice-cream scoop to drop some of the mixture onto a pre-greased baking tray.

6. Bake for 15 minutes at 325 degrees.

7. Cool on a wire rack and serve.

Nutritional Information

Calories: 211

Carbohydrates: 30.8 g

Proteins: 3.4 g

Fats: 9.2 g

40. Three Ingredient Chocolate Chip Cookies

Simple, easy and healthy cookie fix.

Serves 7

Ingredients

1 Cup Rolled Oats

1/4 Cup Chocolate Chips

2 Over Ripe Bananas

Procedure

1. Mash the bananas with a fork.

2. Mix with chocolate chips and rolled oats

3. Line cookies on a baking tray.

4. Bake for 15 minutes at 350 degrees or until the cookies are golden brown.

5. Allow to cool. Do not touch them while they are cooling.

6. When completely cool, remove and enjoy!

Nutritional Information

Calories: 76

Carbohydrates: 11.5 g

Proteins: 2 g

Fats: 2.5 g

41. Vegan Oreos

This is a dream recipe for many. If you are a fan of Oreos, you can recreate this homemade vegan-friendly version.

Serves 10

<u>Ingredients</u>

2 Cups Sugar

1 1/3 Cup Cocoa Powder

1 Cup Coconut Milk

1/4 Cup Water

1 Teaspoon Vanilla Extract

1/4 Teaspoon Salt

3 Flax Eggs

For filling:

2 3/4 Cups Icing Sugar

1 Cup Coconut Butter

3/4 Teaspoon Vanilla Extract

Procedure

1. Sift together the dry ingredients for the cookies.

2. In another bowl, combine the wet ingredients.

3. Pour the wet ingredients into the dry ingredients and form a crumbly dough. Adjust the amount of water accordingly.

4. Roll out the dough and cut out cookies using a round cookie cutter.

5. Bake for about 22 minutes at 325 degrees.

6. While they are baking, soften the butter with a fork.

7. Add in sugar and vanilla extract.

8. Take an electric beater and beat the frosting until light and fluffy.

9. Cool the cookies and sandwich the frosting between two cookies.

10. Dunk in milk and enjoy!

Nutritional Information

Calories: 361

Carbohydrates: 80.6 g

Proteins: 2.6 g

Fats: 7.2 g

Candies

42. Simple 3 Ingredient Chocolate Bars

Sometimes a long list of ingredients can be tiresome and exhausting. First there's the task of collecting them all and then you have to measure all of them out. It is such a hassle. To make things easier, we have a simple recipe that uses just 3 ingredients and yields a simple chocolate bar just like the one you get at a store.

Serves 4-5

Ingredients

1/4 Cup Melted Coconut Oil

1/4 Cup Unsweetened Cocoa Powder

3 Tablespoons Maple Syrup

Procedure

1. Whisk together all three ingredients in a bowl. Make sure that the mixture is smooth and there are no powder lumps.

2. For the best, most commercial looking results you'll need chocolate bar moulds but even if you don't have them something shallow will work.

3. Spread the mixture as thinly as possible onto your surface of choice.

4. Transfer to a freezer and freeze overnight.

5. Break a piece and pop into your mouth as needed.

Nutritional Information

Calories: 21

Carbohydrates: 5.2 g

Proteins: 0.4 g

Fats: 0.3 g

43. Dark Chocolate Truffles

It is hard to resist when goodness comes in small bite sized packages. This is one of those treats. The truffles are easy to make and even easier to eat. You can present them at parties and dinners to impress the guests or just make them for yourself and eat them all up. Both options sound good to me!

Serves 6-8

Ingredients

1 1/4 Cup Grated Dark (at least 70%) chocolate

1/4 Cup Powdered Hazelnuts

7 Tablespoons Coconut Milk

1/2 Teaspoon Vanilla Extract

Procedure

1. In a small saucepan, heat the coconut milk until it just begins to simmer.
2. Take off heat and immediately add the grated dark chocolate. It should be very finely grated.
3. Cover the pan, wrap it with a towel and allow to sit for about 5 minutes.
4. Then slowly remove the lid, add in vanilla extract and gently stir the mixture so that all the chocolate is melted.
5. Allow to cool while covered.
6. When the pan can be touched by a naked hand, uncover and transfer to refrigerator.
7. Allow to chill for about 3 hours.
8. After 3 hours, insert a knife in the middle. If it comes out clean, your mixture is ready.
9. Use a small scoop to take out some of the mixture and roll it into balls.

10. Roll in powdered hazelnuts and line on a plate.

11. Serve and enjoy!

Nutritional Information

Calories: 89

Carbohydrates: 9.7 g

Proteins: 1.3 g

Fats: 5 g

44. Chocolate Jelly

Who would have thought of combining these two amazing ingredients? Surprisingly these both work very well together.

Serves 10

Ingredients

1 Cup Water

1/3 Cup Sugar

1/4 Cup Brewed Espresso

1/4 Cup Cocoa Powder

1 1/2 Tablespoon Agar Flakes

A Pinch of Salt

Procedure

1. In a saucepan, combine together water and agar flakes. Allow to sit for about 15 minutes.

2. Then put on heat and bring to a boil.

3. Lower the heat and allow to simmer until all the agar flakes have dissolved.

4. Add in all the other ingredients apart from the espresso. If you add in the espresso now, the coffee will burn and become bitter.

5. Take off the heat, add espresso and pour into small cups, glasses or moulds.

6. Freeze until set.

7. Pop out and enjoy!

Nutritional Information

Calories: 30

Carbohydrates: 7.8 g

Proteins: 0.4 g

Fats: 0.3 g

45. Jam Filled Chocolates

Candies with fillings are always the best. To me, the filling is a tiny surprise that you get as you bite into it.

Serves 10

Ingredients

For the Jam:

1 Cup Dried Cherries

3 Tablespoons Water

1 Tablespoon Pure Maple Syrup

1 Teaspoon Vanilla Extract

For the Chocolates:

1/2 Cup Raw Cocoa

1/2 Cup Cocoa Butter or Coconut Oil

1/4 Cup Maple Syrup

1/2 Teaspoon Vanilla Extract

Procedure

1. Add all the jam ingredients to a food processor and blend until smooth or slightly chunky depending on your preference.

2. Add the water slowly and not at once or otherwise the jam might get too liquid.

3. Scrape off and store in a jar. You can also use this jam as a spread on toast.

4. Melt the cocoa butter or coconut oil and whisk in the other chocolate ingredients until smooth batter forms.

5. Take paper muffin cups and fill the half way with the mixture.

6. Freeze for about 3-4 hours.

7. Remove and add a layer of the cherry jam.

8. Add another layer of the chocolate mixture and return to freezer for a few more hours.

9. Remove from the freezer.

10. Serve chilled.

Nutritional Information

Calories: 131

Carbohydrates: 9.1 g

Proteins: 0.8 g

Fats: 11.5 g

45. Pine Bark Chocolate

Can you imagine something that resembles a wood bark but tastes like bittersweet chocolate? Ingenious!

Serves 16-18

Ingredients

27 Vegan Salty Crackers

1 Cup Date Paste

1/2 Cup Semi-Sweet Chocolate Chips

1/2 Cup Chopped Pecans

2 Tablespoons Maple Syrup

1 Tablespoon Coconut Oil

1 Teaspoon Vanilla Extract

Procedure

1. Line a baking pan with parchment paper.

2. Spread crackers on the entire surface.

3. In a small saucepan, melt coconut oil.

4. Add maple syrup, vanilla extract and date paste.

5. Bring to a boil and then turn off the heat.

6. Spread the mixture over the crackers.

7. Quickly add a full layer of chocolate chips.

8. Wait until the chocolate melts from the heat of the date mixture underneath.

9. Sprinkle with pecans. Press them into the chocolate.

10. Refrigerate until completely hard.

11. Cut and serve.

Nutritional Information

Calories: 136

Carbohydrates: 21.2 g

Proteins: 1.8 g

Fats: 4.3 g

46. Chocolate Dipped Biscotti

The base of this biscotti is zingy and slightly nutty due to the inclusion or orange zest and almonds while the chocolate coating gives it a novel touch. You will surely love this treat for breakfast and as dessert.

Serves 15

Ingredients

1 3/4 Cups Flour

3/4 Cup Coconut Palm Sugar

3/4 Cup Dark Chocolate Chips

1/2 Cup Cornmeal

1/2 Cup Coconut Oil

1/2 Cup Pumpkin Puree

1/2 Cup Chopped Almonds

1 1/2 Teaspoon Baking Powder

1 Teaspoon Orange Zest

1 Teaspoon Vanilla Extract

A Pinch of Salt

Procedure

1. Mix together all the dry ingredients (apart from chocolate chips)

2. Mix together all the wet ingredients in another bowl.

3. Fold the wet ingredients into the dry ingredients and mix well to make a dough.

4. Take about golf sized balls of dough and elongate and flatten them.

5. Line on a baking tray.

6. Bake for 25 minutes at 350 degrees. Then flip over and bake for another 15-20 minutes.

7. In the meanwhile, melt the chocolate chips over a double boiler.

8. Allow the baked biscotti to cool and dip them halfway into melted chocolate.

9. Place over parchment paper and cool until the chocolate has

hardened.

10. Enjoy!

Nutritional Information

Calories: 181

Carbohydrates: 19.9 g

Proteins: 3 g

Fats: 10.8 g

47. Vegan Chocolate "Eggs"

You must have had this candy that is chocolate on the outside and egg imitation sweet dough on the inside. This recipe is a creation of that without any real eggs of course.

Serves 15

Ingredients

3 Cups Sugar

1/2 Cup Corn Syrup

1/4 Cup Vegan Butter

1 Tablespoons Coconut Oil

2 Teaspoons Vanilla Extract

1/4 Teaspoon Sea Salt

Chocolate Chips (as needed)

Red and Yellow Food Colour

Procedure

1. Fluff together corn syrup and vegan butter until light.

2. Stir in sugar slowly until completely dissolved.

3. Add in vanilla extract and salt.

4. Split the mixture (into two). Add two drops yellow and one drop red food colouring to one-half. Leave the other white.

5. Transfer to a freezer and freeze for about 2 hours.

6. After two hours, press about a ball sized piece of white dough into a muffin pan.

7. Press a yellow piece in the centre of it.

8. When done, transfer to the freezer again.

9. In the meanwhile, melt the chocolate chips with coconut oil over a double boiler. Add in the vanilla extract.

10. After about an hour, take out your "eggs"

11. Using a fork, dip them in your chocolate and replace in the muffin pan.

12. Freeze until the chocolate has hardened.

13. Enjoy!

Nutritional Information

Calories: 188

Carbohydrates: 47.9 g

Proteins: 0 g

Fats: 0.9 g

48. Chocolate Covered Popcorns

If there can be caramel popcorn, then why not chocolate popcorn?

Serves 4

Ingredients

8 Cups Popped Popcorn

1/2 Cup Grated Dark Chocolate

2 Tablespoon Coconut Oil

Procedure

1. Melt coconut oil in a pan.
2. Melt chocolate in a microwave.
3. Mix the coconut oil and melted chocolate.
4. Drizzle the mixture over the popcorn.
5. Toss to mix.
6. Spread on a baking tray to allow the chocolate to solidify.
7. Put on a movie and enjoy!

Nutritional Information

Calories: 233

Carbohydrates: 24.9 g

Proteins: 3.7 g

Fats: 13.8 g

49. White Chocolate Bar

White chocolate is considered to be a delicacy because it is comparatively rare. Not everyone appreciates white chocolate, but if you do, here is a recipe for the simplest white chocolate bar.

Yields 1 Bar

Ingredients

1 Cup Cocoa Butter

1/4 Cup Coconut Oil

1 1/2 Tablespoon Cashew Butter

1 Tablespoon Light Agave Nectar

1 Teaspoon Vanilla Extract

A Pinch of Salt

Procedure

1. You will need a chocolate bar mould for this.

2. Melt cocoa butter over a double boiler and add the coconut oil.

3. Dissolve all the other ingredients in it as well.

4. Pour into the mould and allow to cool.

5. Transfer to a freezer and solidify.

6. Break into pieces and enjoy!

Nutritional Information

Calories: 482

Carbohydrates: 0.5 g

Proteins: 0 g

Fats:54.5 g

50. Almond Chocolate and Cherry Crisps

This is an amazing "pop-in-your-mouth" recipe, in which you can pretty much use any crispy ingredients. If you don't like cherries, use chopped blueberries or any other berries instead. This recipe is very customizable.

Serves 18

Ingredients

1 1/2 Cup Rice Krispies

1 Cup Chocolate Chips

3/4 Cup Dried Cherries

1/3 Cup Slivered Almonds

1/2 Teaspoon Vanilla Extract

Procedure

1. Melt chocolate chips over a double boiler.

2. Add all the other ingredients to the melted chocolate and toss.

3. Drop 3 spoonfuls of mixture onto a baking tray and chill in the freezer.

4. Serve.

Nutritional Information

Calories: 60

Carbohydrates: 5.9 g

Proteins: 1.1 g

Fats: 3.6 g

51. Vegan Kit Kat

Kit Kat is one of the most popular chocolate bars out there. Creamy, dreamy chocolate on the outside, crispy wafer on the inside. It doesn't need any introduction, right? Since Kit Kat is manufactured by Nestle, it is a brand who is the face of milk products. It is not a good option for vegans. However, the fortunate thing is that you can recreate it quite easily without using regular milk.

Serves 1-3

Ingredients

1 Cup Semi-Sweet Chocolate Chips

1 Tablespoon Coconut Oil

12 Vanilla or Chocolate Vegan Wafers

Procedure

1. Melt together chocolate chips and coconut oil over a double boiler or in a microwave.

2. Dip wafers into the chocolate mixture and set on parchment paper.

3. Use a pair of tongs if needed.

4. Allow the chocolate to set.

5. Enjoy!

<u>Nutritional Information</u>

Calories: 146

Carbohydrates: 13.3 g

Proteins: 1.3 g

Fats: 9.9 g

52. Chocolate Peanut Butter Cups

These tiny cups remind me of Reese's. Just a healthier homemade version.

Serves 12

Ingredients

1 Cup Semi-Sweet Chocolate Chips

1/3 Cup Cookie Crumbs

1/2 Cup Icing Sugar

1/2 Cup Peanut Butter

2 Tablespoons Vegan Butter

1 Teaspoon Coconut Oil

Procedure

1. You will need cupcake liners for this.

2. Melt together coconut oil and chocolate chips in a double boiler.

3. Pour about a teaspoon of chocolate mixture into each muffin liner and freeze until set.

4. While you are waiting for step 3 to get done, mix together the rest of the ingredients.

5. Take the liners out of the freezer and fill 3/4 with the peanut butter filling.

6. Fill the remaining top with the chocolate mixture.

7. Return to freezer and freeze until set.

8. Pop out and enjoy!

Nutritional Information

Calories: 129

Carbohydrates: 12.7 g

Proteins: 3 g

Fats: 8.1 g

Fruits and Chocolate

53. Chocolate Covered Cherries

Do you know one of those recipes that look incredibly difficult but are in fact exceedingly simple to make? Well this is one of those recipes. It looks all fancy and exotic but is in fact very simple. So easy that even a child could make it. In fact, it is the perfect recipe to bring the family together. Get your kids in the kitchen with you and have a little family time.

Serves 5-7

<u>Ingredients</u>

1 1/2 Cups Fresh Cherries

1/4 Cup Coconut Oil

1/4 Cup Melted Chocolate

1 Tablespoon Maple Syrup

Procedure

1. In a large bowl, whisk together coconut oil, melted chocolate and maple syrup.

2. Line a baking tray with parchment paper.

3. Pick each cherry, dip it in the mixture and then place it on the baking tray.

4. Line the tray with cherries.

5. Transfer to refrigerator and allow to cool until the chocolate coating hardens.

6. Enjoy this simple treat!

Nutritional Information

Calories: 75

Carbohydrates: 1.9 g

Proteins: 0 g

Fats: 7.8 g

54. Raspberry Hot Chocolate

If you are a fan of fruits and chocolate together then you will love this recipe. It is a fun twist on a traditional recipe. Something new to try and experiment with.

Serves 1

Ingredients

1 Cup Almond Milk

1/4 Cup Dark Chocolate Chips

1 Tablespoon Raspberry Jam

1 Teaspoon Cocoa Powder

Procedure

1. Heat almond milk over low heat.

2. Add raspberry jam and cocoa powder to it. Keep stirring but do not bring to a boil.

3. Melt the chocolate chips over a double boiler and pour in a mug.

4. Turn off the heat and pour half the milk mixture into the chocolate. Stir to ensure that there are no lumps.

5. Then add in the rest of the milk and stir.

6. Enjoy hot!

Nutritional Information

Calories: 746

Carbohydrates: 47. 3 g

Proteins: 7.9 g

Fats: 55.9 g

55. Fruity Chocolaty Oat Bars

Nutrition bars are extremely popular in the modern world. They are convenient, easy to make and remarkably delicious. This makes them a perfect option for anyone looking to eat healthy without having it taste like rabbit food.

Serves 8

Ingredients

1 1/2 Cups Steel Cut Oats

1 1/2 Cups Raspberries

3/4 Cup Whole Wheat Flour

3/4 Cup Chocolate Chips

2/3 Cup Coconut Oil

1/2 Cup Brown Sugar

5 Tablespoons Raspberry Jam

1/2 Teaspoon Vanilla Extract

1/4 Teaspoon Salt

1/4 Teaspoon Baking Powder

Procedure

1. In a large bowl, combine together oats, wheat flour, brown sugar, coconut oil, salt and baking powder.

2. The mixture should stick together but should not be gooey.

3. Line a baking pan with parchment paper and press the mixture onto the bottom and to the sides as well.

4. Bake at 375 degrees Fahrenheit until the crust begins to brown.

5. While it is baking, in a small bowl mix together raspberries, raspberry jam and vanilla extract.

6. Mash using a fork until mushy.

7. Pour this mixture into the middle of the crust and cover with chocolate chips.

8. Bake for another 22 minutes.

9. Allow to cool and slice.

10. Store and serve as needed.

Nutritional Information

Calories: 420

Carbohydrates: 48.6 g

Proteins: 4.8 g

Fats: 24.1 g

56. Cupped Chocolate Apricot Truffles

When you bite into these little truffles, the apricot gives off the texture of jelly. Even though it tastes like jelly, it is much healthier. You are getting your dose of fruit in the form of candy!

Serves 20

Ingredients

3 Cups Chocolate Chips

1 Cup Almond Milk

1 Cup Dried Apricots

3/4 Cup Melted Chocolate

1/4 Cup Chopped Pecans

1 Tablespoon Cocoa Powder

Procedure

1. In a food processor, add milk and cocoa. Blend until smooth.

2. Add in the melted chocolate and blend again.

3. Add in the apricots and pulse. Chop the apricots into small pieces but don't puree them.

4. Pour into a bowl and refrigerate overnight. In the morning, it will have a truffle like consistency.

5. Prepare muffin liners.

6. Melt chocolate chips over a double boiler.

7. Heap about a spoonful of the melted chocolate into each muffin liner.

8. Freeze for about half an hour to set the chocolate.

9. Take out and add a layer of the truffle mixture. Smooth the top using a spoon.

10. Freeze for another hour.

11. Take out and enjoy!

Nutritional Information

Calories: 167

Carbohydrates: 16.6 g

Proteins: 2.4 g

Fats: 10.4 g

57. Chocolate Dipped Strawberries

The perfect summertime treat to enjoy on a lazy afternoon or after a barbeque. Easy to make. Easy to eat. A simple pleasure in life.

Serves 10

<u>Ingredients</u>

20 Fresh and Ripe Strawberries

1/2 Cup Melted Dark Chocolate

2 Tablespoons Vegan Butter

2 Tablespoons Agave Nectar (if your chocolate is already sweet, don't add this)

1/2 Teaspoon Strawberry Essence

<u>Procedure</u>

1. Melt vegan butter in a pan and add in the melted chocolate, strawberry essence and agave nectar.

2. Remove from heat.

3. Pick each strawberry by the leaves and dip completely in the chocolate mixture.

4. Lay on parchment paper.

5. Wait for the chocolate to harden.

6. Enjoy!

Nutritional Information

Calories: 28

Carbohydrates: 1.9 g

Proteins: 0.2 g

Fats: 2.3 g

58. Chocolate Chip Filled Banana Bread Bites

The title is pretty much self-explanatory. If you love chocolate chip banana bread but do not like the hassle of making the whole loaf, then this is a really neat recipe for you.

Serves 5

Ingredients

1/2 Cup Rolled Oats

1/4 Cup Coconut Flour

2 Tablespoons Chocolate Chips

4 Pitted Dates

1 Ripe Banana

Procedure

1. Add the ingredients, minus the chocolate chips, to a food processor.

2. Blend until smooth mixture forms.

3. Pour into a bowl and fold in the chocolate chips.

4. Make small golf sized balls by hand.

5. Place in the freezer for 2-3 hours.

6. Serve.

<u>Nutritional Information</u>

Calories: 93

Carbohydrates: 18.4 g

Proteins: 1.8 g

Fats: 1.9 g

59. Chocolate Amoretti Peaches

These broiled peaches are a perfect mixture between crisp tartness and mushy sweetness. Perfect for a chocolate fix on a vegan diet.

Serves 8

Ingredients

1/2 Cup Crushed Chocolate Cookies

1/4 Cup Grated Dark Chocolate

2 Tablespoons Brown Sugar

8 Teaspoons Vegan Butter

4 Large Peaches

Cooking Spray

Procedure

1. Preheat a broiler.

2. Divide each peach into four pieces and remove the centres to form a boat like shape.

3. Mix together cookie crumbs and sugar in a bowl.

4. Fill the peaches with this mixture and top with vegan butter and chocolate shavings.

5. Arrange in a dish and broil until vegan butter and chocolate melts.

6. Cool and enjoy!

<u>Nutritional Information</u>

Calories: 543

Carbohydrates: 102.5 g

Proteins: 8.9 g

Fats: 14.6 g

Handy Snacks

60. Chocolate Coated Raisins

These make for great on-the-go treats. You can just pick a handful and pop them into your mouth. The raisins are naturally sweet so that eliminates the need for any additional sweetener.

Serves 4-5

Ingredients

1 1/2 Cups Raisins

1/4 Cup Vegan Chocolate Chips

1/2 Tablespoon Coconut Oil

Procedure

1. Melt the chocolate chips over a double boiler.

2. Add in the coconut oil and mix until both are homogenous.

3. Remove from heat and add in the raisins.

4. Mix well so that each one is coated.

5. Spread on a baking tray lined with parchment paper and allow to air dry.

6. When dry, the coating will be crisp.

7. Store in an airtight jar and enjoy!

Nutritional Information

Calories: 158

Carbohydrates: 27.6 g

Proteins: 1.5 g

Fats: 2.4 g

61. Super Balls

This is the most nutritious type of dessert that you can imagine. It is primarily made out of healthy nuts and seeds. The best part is that it is a lavish treat.

Serves 10

Ingredients

1 1/2 Cups Pitted Dates

1/2 Cup Shredded Coconut

1/2 Cup Cocoa Powder

1/4 Cup Ground Flaxseeds

1/4 Cup Chia Seeds

1/4 Cup Sunflower Seeds

1/4 Cup Cocoa Nibs

2 Tablespoons Coconut Oil

1/2 Tablespoon Warm Water

Procedure

1. Add the dates and warm water to a food processor and process until smooth paste forms. Add more water if needed.

2. Now add in all the other ingredients to make a dough.

3. Use this mixture to form small round balls. Coat them in cocoa powder and lay on a baking tray.

4. Transfer this tray to a freezer and freeze overnight.

5. Add to an airtight jar and keep in the refrigerator.

6. Enjoy!

Nutritional Information

Calories: 144

Carbohydrates: 24 g

Proteins: 2.3 g

Fats: 4 g

62. Chocolate Fudge Pops

Fudge pops that can be frozen and popped (pun totally intended) out of the freezer at any time.

Serves 12

Ingredients

1 1/2 Cups Soy Yogurt

1 1/2 Cups Chocolate Chips

1 Cup Almond Milk

2 Teaspoons Vanilla Extract

Procedure

1. Melt the chocolate chips over a double boiler.

2. Add in the milk and stir to form chocolate milk.

3. Pour the mixture into a saucepan and bring to a boil. Then reduce the

heat and simmer for 5 minutes.

4. In a bowl, combine together yogurt and vanilla extract.

5. Remove the mixture from heat and allow to cool.

7. Mix in with the yogurt.

8. Take a muslin cloth and strain the liquid.

9. Take the liquid and pour into popsicle moulds.

10. Put in the freezer until frozen solid.

11. Enjoy!

Nutritional Information

Calories: 184

Carbohydrates: 16.8 g

Proteins: 3.3 g

Fats: 11.8 g

63. Pumpkin Chocolate Rounds

Pumpkin is a fall staple. There are pumpkin pies, pumpkin spiced lattes and pumpkin scented candles. It is a festive treat. You can bring that seasonal festivity to your food as well by cooking something other than the typical pumpkin pie. These rounds are simple, delicious and capture the essence of fall perfectly.

Serves 8

Ingredients

1 Cup Coconut Butter

1 Cup Pumpkin Puree

1/2 Cup Cocoa Powder

1/2 Cup Agave Nectar (you can also use honey but it has a very distinctive flavour)

1 Teaspoon Vanilla Extract

2 Pinches of Salt

Procedure

1. Line round candy moulds with parchment paper. You can also use a muffin tray but it won't yield perfect rounds.
2. In a large bowl, mix together all the ingredients until homogenous.
3. Pour into moulds and freeze overnight.
4. Pop one out and enjoy as needed!

Nutritional Information

Calories: 24

Carbohydrates: 5.5 g

Proteins: 1.3 g

Fats: 0.8 g

64. Chocolate Banana Bites

Chocolate and bananas are a great traditional combo; and a vegan delight

Serves 7-10

Ingredients

3 Cups of Assorted Coatings (sprinkles, nuts, granola, shredded coconut etc. are just a few options)

2 Cups Grated Chocolate

2 Tablespoons Coconut Oil

3 Bananas

Procedure

1. Peel the bananas and slice them in rounds.
2. Melt the chocolate over a double boiler and add in the coconut oil.

Mix well.

3. Take off heat.

4. Use a fork to pick up the banana slices and dip them into the chocolate one by one.

5. After dipping in chocolate, roll the banana in the coating of choice and line on parchment paper.

6. Place in the freezer for 3-4 hours.

7. Enjoy!

Nutritional Information

Calories: 335

Carbohydrates: 40.1 g

Proteins: 4.2 g

Fats: 18.3 g

65. Coconut Filled Chocolate Balls

Coconut is a great chocolate filing, which inspired me to recreate this combination myself.

Serves 6

<u>Ingredients</u>

2 oz. Dark Chocolate

1/2 Cup Shredded Coconut

1/8 Cup Coconut Oil

1 Tablespoons Maple Syrup

1/2 Teaspoon Vanilla Extract

<u>Procedure</u>

1. In a bowl combine together coconut, coconut oil, maple syrup and vanilla extract.

2. Mix well.

3. Make small balls and place on a plate.

4. Place the plate in the fridge for about half an hour.

5. In the meanwhile, melt the chocolate over a double boiler.

6. Using a fork, dip the coconut balls into the melted chocolate and set on a parchment paper.

7. Wait until the chocolate hardens.

8. Enjoy!

Nutritional Information

Calories: 123

Carbohydrates: 8.9 g

Proteins: 0.9 g

Fats: 9.6 g

Ice-Cream

66. Mocha Ice-cream

Most coffee shops either sell mocha or a mocha shake. My favorite is mocha ice-cream shake. It is the perfect blend of coffee and chocolate flavors. Once you can perfect the ice-cream, making the shake is easy breezy.

Serves 4

Ingredients

1 1/2 Cups Almond Milk

1 Cup Cashews (raw and unsalted)

1/2 Cup Coconut Palm Sugar

1/4 Cup Cocoa Powder

2 Tablespoons Raw Agave Nectar

2 Teaspoons Instant Coffee

1 Teaspoon Vanilla Extract

A Pinch of Salt

Procedure

1. Soak the cashews in water for about 5-6 hours.
2. Drain and add to a blender with all the other ingredients.
3. Blend until smooth and creamy.
4. Add to an ice-cream maker and churn until firm yet soft.
5. Transfer to a container and freeze.
6. Scoop out and enjoy!

Nutritional Information

Calories: 335

Carbohydrates: 15.4 g

Proteins: 6.6 g

Fats: 30.4 g

67. Peanut Butter, Banana and Chocolate Ice-Cream

Three of my favourite things in one!

This homemade ice cream is dairy free (of course) and has a great nutty flavour (thanks to the peanut butter). It is also surprisingly healthy because it has a fruit base. A great treat for some special occasions or whenever you want to treat yourself.

Serves 2

Ingredients

6 Pitted Dates

2 Frozen Bananas

2 Tablespoons Soy Milk

2 Tablespoons Cocoa Powder

2 Tablespoons Peanut Butter

A Pinch of Salt

Procedure

1. The bananas need to be frozen overnight or otherwise this won't work.

2. Break the frozen banana into small pieces and add to a food processor.

3. Start slow and begin blending. If you go too fast, it will just become mushy like baby food. Instead go slow and slowly, it will start getting the consistency of a fluffy ice-cream.

4. In a blender or another food processor, blend together all the rest of the ingredients.

5. Now slowly add the mixture to the bananas and mix evenly.

6. Process a little if needed.

7. Scoop out and freeze for about 15 minutes.

8. Serve immediately.

Nutritional Information

Calories: 184

Carbohydrates: 25.8 g

Proteins: 6.1 g

Fats: 9.1 g

68. Banana Split

Among my favourite childhood memories is going to a small ice-cream shop with my mom and ordering a huge banana split. Made me feel so grown up! Now that I have actually grown up, I recreate that memory by making my own banana split.

Serves 1

Ingredients

1 Large Banana

1 Scoop Vegan Mocha Ice-Cream

1 Scoop Vegan Strawberry Ice-Cream

1 Scoop Vegan Vanilla Ice-Cream

3 Tablespoons Chocolate Syrup

1 Tablespoon Chopped Walnuts

1 Tablespoon Chopped Slivered Almonds

1 Tablespoon Chopped Pecans

1 Glazed Cherry

Procedure

1. Slice the banana lengthwise and place in a boat dish.

2. Place the three scoops of ice-cream lengthwise.

3. Top with chopped walnuts, pecans and almonds.

4. Drizzle generously with chocolate syrup.

5. Place a cherry on the middle ice-cream scoop.

6. Take a spoon and dig in!

Nutritional Information

Calories: 361

Carbohydrates: 69.7 g

Proteins: 5.8 g

Fats: 8.7 g

Shakes and Smoothies

69. Crackpot Hot Chocolate

Hot Chocolate is a staple winter treat. There is nothing like a steaming mug of hot chocolate and a good book on a chilly winter evening. While you are reading, you can add the ingredients to a crackpot and forget all about it. Later, your steaming, yummy mug of hot chocolate would be ready for you to enjoy. It is very easy!

Serves 5

Ingredients

5 Cups Almond Milk

1 Cup Warm Water

1/2 Cup Cocoa Powder

1/2 Cup Sugar

Procedure

1. Mix together all the ingredients in a saucepan or a jug.

2. Add to a ready crackpot.

3. Cook on high for 2 hours.

4. Pour into cups and enjoy!

Nutritional Information

Calories: 646

Carbohydrates: 38 g

Proteins: 7.1 g

Fats: 51.4 g

70. Mocha Ice cream Shake

This is an amazing shake that smells and tastes just like the one you get at any popular cafe.

Serves 2

Ingredients

4 Scoops Mocha Ice-cream

2/3 Cups Almond Milk

1/2 Cup Grated Dark Chocolate

1/2 Tablespoon Dark Cocoa Powder

1 Teaspoon Instant Coffees

1 Teaspoon Vanilla Extract

1/8 Teaspoon Almond Extract

Whipped Coconut Cream (optional)

Procedure

1. Take two tall glasses and add one scoop of ice-cream per glass. Transfer to a freezer.

2. In a blender, combine together all the ingredients (apart from whipped cream and save half the grated chocolate)

3. Blend until smooth and creamy.

4. Retrieve the glasses from the freezer and pour the milkshake over the ice-cream.

5. Top with whipped cream and sprinkle grated chocolate on top.

6. Enjoy!

Nutritional Information

Calories: 416

Carbohydrates: 29.7 g

Proteins: 5 g

Fats: 31.5 g

71. White Hot Chocolate

There are many people that actually prefer white chocolate to regular dark or milk chocolate. Usually it is thought that white chocolate is a no-go on a vegan diet because it is mostly milk based. However, if you are a white chocolate lover, there is good news. This vegan recipe nearly replicates the taste of white chocolate in a creamy hot drink.

Serves 1

Ingredients

1 Cup Almond Milk

2 Tablespoons Vegan Cream

1/2 Teaspoon Vanilla Extract

Stevia to Taste

A Pinch of Powdered Cinnamon

A Pinch of Salt

Procedure

1. In a mug, whisk together cream, vanilla extract, salt, stevia and some milk.

2. When frothy, add in the rest of the almond milk.

3. Sprinkle cinnamon on top.

4. Microwave for about a minute.

5. Enjoy warm!

Nutritional Information

Calories: 558

Carbohydrates: 13.6 g

Proteins: 5.5 g

Fats: 57.2 g

72. Almond Avocado Chocolate Smoothie

Did you know that consuming other foods with avocado increases nutrient absorption? That's right. It acts like a nutrient magnet. Inside your gut. This makes avocados the perfect ingredient to add to health smoothies. There's also the added bonus that they lend the smoothie a very rich, creamy texture.

Serves 2

Ingredients

1 Cup Almond Milk

1 Tablespoons Cocoa Nibs

1 Tablespoon Almond Butter

1/2 Tablespoon Maple Syrup

1/4 Teaspoon Vanilla Extract

1 Small Diced Avocado

A Pinch of Salt

A Handful of Kale or Spinach

Procedure

1. Add all the ingredients to a high-speed power blender.

2. If you do not have a power blender, add ingredients one by one.

3. Blend until smooth and creamy.

4. Pour over ice and enjoy!

Nutritional Information

Calories: 546

Carbohydrates: 20.1 g

Proteins: 6.3 g

Fats: 52.7 g

73. Chocolate Spinach Smoothie

Let's be honest, spinach is a hard vegetable to eat. It is bland in taste and the texture isn't that great either. For that reason, I find it best to disguise it in my smoothies. If the flavours are strong enough, you can't feel or taste the spinach at all.

Serves 1

Ingredients

1 1/2 Cup Chopped Fresh Spinach

1 Cup Soy Milk

1/2 Cup Vanilla Soy Yogurt

1/2 Cup Blueberries

1 1/2 Tablespoons Dark Cocoa Powder

1 Teaspoon Vanilla Essence

1 Banana

Sugar to Taste

Procedure

1. Add all the ingredients to a high-speed power blender.

2. Blend until smooth and creamy.

3. Pour over ice and enjoy!

Nutritional Information

Calories: 303

Carbohydrates: 55.5 g

Proteins: 11.1 g

Fats: 5.1 g

74. Cookie Dough Shake

Nothing like a shake to deal with a hot day!

Serves 1

Ingredients

1 Cup Almond Milk

1/4 Cup Vegan Vanilla Protein Powder

1/4 Cup Rolled Oats

1 Tablespoon Sugar

1/8 Teaspoon Baking Soda

1/8 Teaspoon Sea Salt

6 Drops Maple Extract

A Handful of Chocolate Chips

Procedure

1. Add almond milk and rolled oats to a blender.

2. Blend until smooth and there are no flakes left.

3. Add the sugar, baking soda, sea salt, maple extract and protein powder.

4. Blend until homogenized.

5. Pour into a cup and top with chocolate chips.

6. Use a straw to drink as the smoothie will be thick.

Nutritional Information

Calories: 337

Carbohydrates: 19.7 g

Proteins: 4.1 g

Fats: 29.3 g

75. Cacao and Maca Smoothie

Cacao powder is an unrefined form of cocoa that contains much more antioxidants than just regular cocoa. So this smoothie is highly energizing, anti-aging and simply delicious.

Serves 2

Ingredients

4 Ice Cubes

2 Bananas

1 1/5 Cups Soy Milk

2 Tablespoons Cacao Powder

2 Tablespoons Maca Powder

A Pinch of Ground Cinnamon

Procedure

1. Add all the ingredients to a high-speed power blender (apart from ice cubes).

2. Blend until smooth. It won't require much effort or time.

3. Add in the ice cubes. You can also use water but using ice cubes chills the drink.

4. Give one last whirl.

5. Pour into a tall glass and enjoy!

Nutritional Information

Calories: 713

Carbohydrates: 41.7 g

Proteins: 7.3 g

Fats: 55.9 g

76. Spicy Chocolate Smoothie

Warm and spicy are not the words you traditionally associate with chocolate but in this recipe, this combination surprisingly works really well. The bitter sweetness of chocolate grounds the spices. As a result, you get a very warm and cosy drink.

Serves 1

Ingredients

2/3 Cup Cashew Milk

1 Tablespoon Chocolate Chips

1 Tablespoon Almond Butter

1 Tablespoon Cacao Powder

1/2 Teaspoon Ground Cinnamon

A Pinch of Cayenne Pepper

A Pinch of Salt

1 Banana

Procedure

1. Add the milk and almond butter to the blender. Blend until the almond butter is completely dissolved.

2. Add in the cocoa powder, spices and banana.

3. Blend until smooth.

4. Add in the chocolate chips and pulse to break into small pieces.

5. Pour in a cup and microwave for about 30 seconds.

6. Enjoy warm.

Nutritional Information

Calories: 266

Carbohydrates: 37.1 g

Proteins: 5.6 g

Fats: 12.6 g

77. Chocolate Raspberry Smoothie

This tangy sweet smoothie is perfect for warm spring and summer mornings when you want something refreshing yet filling and nutritious.

Serves 2

Ingredients

1 1/2 Cup Almond Milk

1 Cup Frozen Raspberries

1/4 Cup Cocoa Powder

1 Tablespoon Coconut Oil

1 Teaspoon Vanilla Extract

7 Dates

1 Banana

Procedure

1. Soak dates in water for 10 minutes to soften them up.

2. Add dates, raspberries, banana and coconut oil to a food processor.

3. Blend to make a puree.

4. Add in the milk, cocoa powder and vanilla extract.

5. Blend until smooth.

6. Pour over ice and enjoy!

Nutritional Information

Calories: 766

Carbohydrates: 84.1 g

Proteins: 8.3 g

Fats: 44.8 g

78. Chocolate and Peanut Butter Power Smoothie

This smoothie is so nutritious that it can almost replace a meal. Flax and chia seeds are known as super foods that give this drink an extra zing. In addition to that, there is also spinach. All of this is wrapped up in a neat little package (or should I say glass?)

Serves 2

Ingredients

1 Cup Soy Milk

1 Cup Spinach

2 Tablespoons Cacao Powder

1 Tablespoon Peanut Butter

1 Tablespoon Ground Flaxseeds

1 Tablespoon Chia Seeds

1 Teaspoon Maca Powder

1/4 Teaspoon Ground Cinnamon

2 Dates

1 Banana

Procedure

1. Add all the ingredients to a power blender.

2. Blend until smooth. Make sure that seeds are finely powdered and invisible in the drink or otherwise they will annoy you while drinking.

3. If you don't have a power blender, powder the seeds beforehand and then add to the drink.

4. When smooth, pour over ice.

5. Serve chilled.

Nutritional Information

Calories: 422

Carbohydrates: 29.7 g

Proteins: 6.7 g

Fats: 26.5 g

79. Chocolate Chip Mint Smoothie

Chocolate mints are a great way to freshen up after dinner. Well this has a similar concept but just in a drink form.

Serves 2

Ingredients

2 Cup Almond Milk

2 Tablespoon Cacao Powder

2 Teaspoon Maple Syrup

2 Teaspoon Cocoa Nibs

24 Dates

14 Mint Leaves

Procedure

1. Add milk, cacao powder, maple syrup, mint leaves and pitted dates to a power blender.

2. Blend until smooth.

3. Pour over ice and top with cocoa nibs.

4. Serve.

Nutritional Information

Calories: 425

Carbohydrates: 46.2 g

Proteins: 4 g

Fats: 25.4 g

80. Almond Coconut Mocha

Almond, coconut, chocolate and coffee all in one? Sounds too good to be true

Serves 1

Ingredients

1/2 Cup Almond Milk

1/2 Cup Coconut Milk

1/3 Cup Chopped Almonds

2 Tablespoons Cocoa Powder

1 Tablespoon Instant Coffee

Stevia to Taste

Procedure

1. Add all the ingredients to a blender and blend until smooth and frothy.

2. Pour over ice and enjoy chilled.

3. Alternatively, you can also heat it and enjoy it warm. It works great both ways.

Nutritional Information

Calories: 759

Carbohydrates: 26 g

Proteins: 14.2 g

Fats: 52.8 g

81. Chocolate Avocado Smoothie

Nobody can sing enough praises for avocado. I sometimes think that maybe it was dropped from heavens for the benefit of mankind.

Serves 1

Ingredients

1/3 Cup Almond Milk

3 Tablespoons Cocoa Powder

1 Tablespoon Maple Syrup

6 Ice Cubes

1 Banana

1/2 Medium Avocado

Procedure

1. Peel and dice the avocado. Peel the banana and slice it.

2. Add all the ingredients apart from ice cubes to a blender.

3. When smooth, add in ice cubes and blend again.

4. Pour into a glass and serve.

Nutritional Information

Calories: 582

Carbohydrates: 62.3 g

Proteins:8 g

Fats: 22.4 g

82. Overnight Oats Smoothie

The mornings are usually such a rushed affair that one doesn't have much time for anything. For this reason, most people including myself like to prepare my smoothies the night before. Like pressing clothes and laying out ingredients for breakfast. This is one such recipe that you can prepare the night before.

Serves 1

Ingredients

1 Cup Almond Milk

1/2 Cup Rolled Oats

2 Tablespoons Hemp Seeds

2 Tablespoons Cocoa Powder

1 Tablespoon Maple Syrup

1/2 Teaspoon Vanilla Extract

Procedure

1. At night, add almond milk, cocoa powder and oats to a mug. Mix well.

2. Leave overnight.

3. The next morning, the oats would have soaked some of the milk and would be mushy.

3. Add all the ingredients to a blender and blend until smooth.

4. Enjoy this quick breakfast.

Nutritional Information

Calories: 395

Carbohydrates: 30.3 g

Proteins: 6.4 g

Fats: 26 g

83. Oreo Blizzard

Oreos are like heaven on earth, whether they are in cookie form or smoothie form.

Serves 2

Ingredients

2/3 Cup Almond Milk

2 Teaspoon Vanilla Extract

8 Vegan Oreos

4 Frozen Bananas

Procedure

1. In a high-speed power blender, add bananas, vanilla extract and almond milk.

2. Blend until you get the consistency of a thick milkshake.

3. Add in the Oreos and blend until the cookies are evenly dispersed in the drink.

4. Pour over ice and use a straw to drink it all up.

Nutritional Information

Calories: 196

Carbohydrates: 5 g

Proteins: 1.8 g

Fats: 19.1 g

Sauces, Syrups and Frostings

84. Chocolate Ganache

This is a multi-purpose sauce. You can use it as frosting, as a spread or even to flavour other recipes. If you are a chocolate lover, then it would be a good idea to have a small jar of some chocolate ganache in your pantry at all times.

Yields 1 Small Mason Jar

Ingredients

1/2 Cup Coconut Palm Sugar

3 Tablespoons Almond Milk

3 Tablespoons Cocoa Powder

2 Tablespoons Almond Butter

2 Tablespoons Tapioca Starch (you can also use sweet potato starch but

tapioca works best)

2 Extra Tablespoons Coconut Palm Sugar

1/4 Teaspoons Vanilla Extract

A Pinch of Salt

Procedure

1. Mix together all the dry ingredients in a bowl.

2. Mix together all the wet ingredients in another bowl.

3. Fold the dry ingredients into the wet ingredients and whisk.

4. Use an electric beater to ensure that everything is smooth and well dissolved.

5. Pour into a sterilized mason jar and screw on the lid. Leave overnight at room temperature.

6. Use as needed. It can be stored at room temperature for about a week.

Nutritional Information

Calories: 182.6

Carbohydrates: 37 g

Proteins: 2.5 g

Fats: 4.5 g

85. Chocolate Avocado Frosting

You can never have enough frosting recipes. I mentioned one earlier and here is another version. The base is avocado, which we now know is nothing short of a super food.

Yields 2 Cups

Ingredients

2 Pitted Medium Avocadoes

1/2 Cup Maple Syrup

1/2 Cup Cocoa Powder

2 Tablespoons Coconut Oil

1 Teaspoon Ground Cinnamon

1/2 Teaspoon Vanilla Extract

Procedure

1. Peel and cube the avocados.

2. Add to a food processor and blend until smooth. Pause in between to scrape off the sides and then blend again.

3. Add in the rest of the ingredients and blend until smooth and creamy.

4. Transfer to a jar and store in the refrigerator.

5. Use as needed.

Nutritional Information

Calories: 52

Carbohydrates: 5.5 g

Proteins: 0.5 g

Fats: 3.7 g

86. Chocolate Fudge Sauce

A fudge sauce can be used as a delicious condiment for a variety of foods. Usually, most recipes have a long list of ingredients and require extensive cooking. Not this one though. It is very easy, needs only three ingredients and can be made in a jiffy.

Yields 1/2 Cup

Ingredients

1/2 Cup Cashew Milk

1/2 Cup Pitted Dates

1 1/2 Tablespoon Cocoa Powder

Procedure

1. Blend together the dates and the milk until smooth.

2. Pour the mixture into a saucepan and bring to a boil.

3. Lower the flame and allow to simmer while stirring periodically.

4. After 10 minutes of simmering, stir in the cocoa powder.

5. Continue to simmer for additional 5 minutes.

6. Remove from heat and pour into a jar.

7. Allow to cool and use as needed.

Nutritional Information

Calories: 13

Carbohydrates: 3.6 g

Proteins: 0.2 g

Fats: 0.1 g

87. Chocolate Syrup

A staple in any pantry.

Yields 1 Mason Jar

<u>Ingredients</u>

1 Can Coconut Milk

1 1/2 Cups Sugar

3/4 Cup Cocoa Powder

1 Tablespoon Vanilla Extract

<u>Procedure</u>

1. Sift together cocoa powder and sugar in a saucepan.

2. Add a little coconut milk. Just enough to make a paste.

3. Then add about half the can of coconut milk.

4. Heat to a roaring boil.

5. Add in the rest of the coconut milk and allow to simmer for 10 minutes. Keep stirring.

6. Remove from heat and stir in the vanilla extract.

7. Allow to cool and pour into a jar or a bottle.

Nutritional Information

Calories: 25

Carbohydrates: 13.5 g

Proteins: 0.5 g

Fats: 0.3 g

88. Caramel Chocolate Sauce

Yields 1 Mason Jar

Ingredients

1 Cup Water

2 Tablespoons Cocoa Powder

1 Teaspoon Vanilla Extract

12 Dates

Procedure

1. Soak the dates in water for 10 minutes.

2. Add all the ingredients to a power blender and blend until smooth.

3. Pour into an airtight jar and store in the refrigerator.

4. Use as needed.

Nutritional Information

Calories: 13

Carbohydrates: 3.2 g

Proteins: 0.2 g

Fats: 0.1 g

89. Simple Chocolate Sauce

You can drizzle this over ice-cream or pancake. Use as a glaze. Eat it on its own.

The options are endless.

Yields 2 1/2 Cups

Ingredients

1 Cup Water

3/4 Cup Cocoa Powder

1/2 Cup Sugar

1/2 Cup Light Corn Syrup

2 Ounces Grated Chocolate

Procedure

1. Mix water, corn syrup, sugar and cocoa powder in a saucepan.

2. Bring to a boil and then allow to simmer.

3. Stir in the chocolate and wait for it to melt. Keep on stirring.

4. Allow to simmer for about 10 minutes.

5. Turn off the heat and let it sit for about 5 minutes before pouring.

6. Cool completely before using.

7. Can be stored up to 10 days.

Nutritional Information

Calories: 25

Carbohydrates: 5.7 g

Proteins: 0.3 g

Fats: 0.5 g

90. Chocolate Dip

This thick and creamy dip are perfect to be used with fruits, crackers or just about anything.

Yields 3 Cups

Ingredients

2 Cup Cashews

1 1/4 Cup Cashew Milk

4 Tablespoons Cocoa Powder

2 Tablespoons Maple Syrup

2 Teaspoons Vanilla Extract

3 Pitted Dates

A Pinch of Salt

Procedure

1. Soak cashews in water overnight.

2. In the morning, combine all the ingredients in a powder blender.

3. Blend until smooth.

4. Store in an airtight container and use as needed.

<u>Nutritional Information</u>

Calories: 40

Carbohydrates: 3.3 g

Proteins: 1 g

Fats: 2.8 g

91. Chocolate Cream "Cheese" Frosting

This is a great example of a "Faux cheese" vegan recipe. In vegan cooking, cashews serve as a perfect replacement for cheese flavour. When done right, they replicate the flavour of parmesan cheese in many dishes.

Yields 1 1/4 Cups

Ingredients

3/4 Cup Raw Cashews

4 Tablespoons Water

3 Tablespoons Maple Syrup

2 Tablespoons Coconut Oil

2 Tablespoon Cocoa Powder

1 Teaspoon Lemon Juice

1 Teaspoon Vanilla Extract

A Pinch of Salt

Procedure

1. Soak cashews in water for about 3 hours. Drain and pat dry.

2. Put them in a food processor and blend until finely powdered.

3. Add in maple syrup, coconut oil, lemon juice and vanilla extract.

4. Mix until a batter begins to form.

5. Pour into a bowl and use an electric beater to whisk the mixture. Add water as needed. The texture should be light and fluffy.

6. When light and fluffy, add in cocoa powder and salt. Mix gently.

7. Use as needed.

Nutritional Information

Calories: 41

Carbohydrates: 3.2 g

Proteins: 0.7 g

Fats: 3.1 g

No Bake Desserts

92. Black Bean Brownie Pops

These make for excellent treats at any party and are surprisingly easy to make. I love them!

Serves 6

Ingredients

2 Cups Boiled and Drained Black Beans

3/4 Cup Chocolate Chips

1/2 Cup Shredded Coconut

5 Tablespoons Cocoa Powder

2 Tablespoons Almond Butter

12 Toothpicks

Procedure

1. In a food processor, combine the black beans, cocoa powder and almond butter.

2. Blend until soft and fudgy.

3. Roll into small balls and line on a baking tray. Stick a toothpick in each of them.

4. Freeze for about 2 hours.

5. In the meanwhile, melt the chocolate chips over a double boiler.

6. Dip each ball into the melted chocolate and roll in shredded coconut.

7. Enjoy!

Nutritional Information

Calories: 180

Carbohydrates: 16.9 g

Proteins: 3.8 g

Fats: 12.1 g

93. Chocolate Peppermint Mousse

Mousse is a decadent dish that is generally associated with eggs. While it is typically made of eggs, there is a vegan version of it that tastes just as good.

Serves 4

Ingredients

1 Can Coconut Cream

1 1/2 Cup Grated Dark Chocolate

1/4 Teaspoon Peppermint Extract

Stevia or any other sweetener as needed

Procedure

1. Chill the coconut cream in the refrigerator overnight. If the coconut cream is not chilled enough, this will not work.

2. In a large bowl, begin beating the cream. Beat until light and fluffy.

3. Add in the sweetener and the peppermint essence. Mix well.

4. Melt chocolate over a double boiler.

5. Fold the chocolate into the whipped coconut cream.

6. Mix well and transfer to bowls.

7. Chill for about an hour before serving.

8. Enjoy!

Nutritional Information

Calories: 270

Carbohydrates: 30 g

Proteins: 3.9 g

Fats: 14.9 g

94. Authentic Chocolate Pudding

Serves 3

Ingredients

2 Cups Coconut Milk

1/2 Cup Soy Milk

1/4 Cup Cocoa Powder

1/4 Cup Grated Dark Chocolate

3 Tablespoons Corn Starch

3/4 Teaspoon Vanilla Extract

Stevia to Taste

A Pinch of Salt

Procedure

1. In a saucepan, combine together coconut milk, cocoa powder and stevia. Stir.

2. In a small bowl, whisk together cornstarch and soy milk. Slowly add this mixture to the coconut milk while continuing to whisk.

3. It will begin to thicken in front of your eyes.

4. Add in the grated chocolates and wait until it is melted.

5. Add the vanilla extract and salt. Stir.

6. Transfer to cups and allow to cool.

7. Freeze overnight. The pudding will thicken as it cools.

8. Enjoy!

Nutritional Information

Calories: 70

Carbohydrates: 12 g

Proteins: 2 g

Fats: 3 g

95. Chocolate Chip Cookie Dough

Rainbows and unicorns and a jar full of cookie dough. Now that's stuff that fantasies are made of. With this recipe though, you can turn the dream of a vegan cookie dough into reality.

Serves 2 (1 if you are crazy about cookie dough)

Ingredients

1 Cup Flour

1/2 Cup Chocolate Chips

1/2 Cup Sugar

1/2 Cup Brown Sugar

1/2 Cup Vegan Butter

2 Tablespoons Almond Milk

2 Teaspoons Vanilla Extract

1/4 Teaspoon Salt

Procedure

1. In a large bowl, combine together vegan butter with both sugars.

2. Whisk until the sugars are completely dissolved and the texture is fluffy.

3. Add in the rest of the ingredients and fold in the chocolate chips.

4. Chill before serving.

Nutritional Information

Calories: 824

Carbohydrates: 159.6 g

Proteins: 10 g

Fats: 16.6 g

96. Peanut Butter and Chocolate Tarts

Chocolate and peanut butter form a classic combination. Followed closely by peanut butter and jelly of course. This particular recipe uses chocolate but if you prefer jam or jelly, you can use that too.

Serves 6

Ingredients

2 Cups Chocolate Cookie Crumbs

2 Cups Chocolate Mousse

1/2 Cup Peanut Butter

3 Tablespoons Chocolate Ganache

2 Tablespoons Coconut Sugar

2 Tablespoons Coconut Oil

Procedure

1. Combine together cookie crumbs, peanut butter, coconut oil and coconut sugar in a large bowl.

2. Take tart moulds and press the mixture onto the bottom.

3. Bake at 375 degrees for 12 minutes or until the crust is golden brown.

4. Allow to cool completely.

5. Fill the tarts with mousse. Use a wet butter knife to smooth it out.

6. Then top with chocolate ganache and place in a freezer.

7. Remove from mould and serve.

Nutritional Information

Calories: 165

Carbohydrates: 4.2 g

Proteins: 5.4 g

Fats: 15.4 g

97. Pistachio Topped Mousse

If you are a mousse lover, here is another easy yet scrumptious recipe for you.

Serves 8

Ingredients

2 Can Coconut Milk

6 Tablespoons Cocoa Powder

5 Tablespoons Maple Syrup

4 Tablespoons Chopped Pistachios

Procedure

1. Place coconut milk into the fridge overnight.

2. When chilled, open the can into a bowl and add in maple syrup and cocoa powder.

3. Your cocoa powder should have a rich taste or otherwise the mousse would be bland.

4. Whip with an electric beater until frothy.

5. Scoop into bowls and top with chopped pistachios.

6. Enjoy!

Nutritional Information

Calories: 52

Carbohydrates: 11.1 g

Proteins: 1.1 g

Fats: 1.4 g

98. No Bake Brownies

Brownies are a delight to eat but a hassle to make. These brownies, however, are easier to make as there is no baking involved. Since there is no baking involved, you don't have to be careful and precise to get the fudgy, chewy texture. It is pretty much a no fail recipe.

Serves 8

Ingredients

1 Cup Rolled Oats

1 Cup Dates

1/2 Cup Chocolate Ganache

1/2 Cup Warm Water

1/4 Cup Cocoa Powder

1/4 Teaspoon Ground Cinnamon

A Pinch of Salt

Procedure

1. Add oats to a food processor and blend until powdered.

2. Soak dates in water for about 20 minutes and then remove the pits.

3. Add all the other ingredients (apart from the ganache) to the food processor and blend until smooth mixture forms.

4. Line a baking pan with parchment paper and press down the mixture onto the pan.

5. Pour the ganache over the top and spread with a butter knife.

6. Freeze for about 4 hours.

7. Cut and serve.

Nutritional Information

Calories: 108

Carbohydrates: 25.1 g

Proteins: 2.4 g

Fats: 1.1 g

99. Quick Chocolate Fudge

Nobody likes a long list of ingredients. So here is a simple fudge recipe that requires just three ingredients.

Serves 36

Ingredients

1 Can Almond Milk

3 Cups Semi-Sweet Chocolate Chips

3/4 Cup Icing Sugar

Procedure

1. Add almond milk in a saucepan and heat until it begins to steam.

2. Add in the sugar and stir until dissolved.

3. Slowly add the chocolate chips while continuing to stir.

4. Line a baking pan with parchment paper.

5. Pour in the mixture.

6. Allow to cool to room temperature.

7. Freeze for about 3 hours or until the fudge has set.

8. Enjoy!

Nutritional Information

Calories: 39

Carbohydrates: 3.2 g

Proteins: 0.3 g

Fats: 3 g

100. Chocolate Custard

This recipe is great because you can eat the custard while warm or store it in the fridge and chill for a dessert serving.

Serves 3

Ingredients

2 Cups Soy Milk

1 Cup Water

6 Tablespoons Sugar

5 Tablespoons Cocoa Powder

4 Tablespoon Corn Flour

1 Teaspoon Vanilla Essence

Procedure

1. Heat soy milk until it begins to steam.

2. Dissolve corn flour in water and set aside.

3. Add sugar and cocoa powder to the steaming milk.

4. Add corn flour and water mixture while stirring slowly.

5. Reduce the heat and allow to simmer.

6. Simmer for about 3-5 minutes or until thick enough.

7. Remove from heat and stir in the vanilla.

8. Pour into cups and chill.

Nutritional Information

Calories: 217

Carbohydrates: 41.9 g

Proteins: 6 g

Fats: 3.2 g

101. Peanut Butter and Chocolate Coated Pretzels

Sometimes having pretzels alone can be a little boring. So here is a recipe to jazz it up a little.

Serves 10

Ingredients

30 Vegan Twist Pretzels

1/2 Cup Dark Chocolate Chips

1/4 Cup Peanut Butter

Procedure

1. Melt chocolate chips in the microwave.

2. Stir in peanut butter until smooth.

3. Dip in one pretzel at a time and line on parchment paper.

4. Refrigerate until set.

5. Enjoy!

Nutritional Information

Calories: 66

Carbohydrates: 5.3 g

Proteins: 2 g

Fats: 4.8 g

Conclusion

Thank you for downloading this book!

I hope this book was able to inspire you to live your vegan lifestyle with some extra fervor. After all, chocolate inspires, doesn't it?

The next step is to select your favorite (all are my favorites by the way), collect ingredients and get cooking! Be it ice cream, shake or cake. Anything that catches your fancy.

Finally, if you enjoyed this book, then I'd like to ask you for a favor.

Would you be kind enough to leave a review for this book on Amazon? It'd be greatly appreciated!

Thank you and good luck!

Appendix

1. *Why Vegan?* Pittsburgh: Vegan Anon, (2016). [online] Available at: http://www.veganoutreach.org/whyvegan/WhyVegan.pdf [Accessed 21 Feb. 2016]. n Outreach, 2000. Web.

2. Anon, (2016). [online] Available at: https://www.friendsofanimals.org/img/Vegan_Starter_Guide.pdf [Accessed 22 Feb. 2016].

3. Anon, (2016). [online] Available at: https://www.vrg.org/nutshell/vegan_nutshell.pdf [Accessed 22 Feb. 2016].

The recipes in this book were inspired by:

Breakfast

1. http://www.runningonrealfood.com/chocolate-chia-protein-pudding/

2. http://www.veganfamilyrecipes.com/2016/01/chocolate-vegan-crepes.html

3. http://chocolatecoveredkatie.com/2012/01/09/better-than-nutella/

4. http://www.pillsbury.com/recipes/slow-cooker-hot-chocolate-oatmeal/ab2df462-0a56-4d6f-a9c2-c6e3262a906f

5. http://www.runningwithspoons.com/2015/02/04/brownie-batter-breakfast-bake/

6. http://blog.pumpup.com/post/vegan-chocolate-waffles-with-blueberry-raspberry-nicecream/

7. http://minimalistbaker.com/chocolate-chip-banana-bread-waffles/

8. http://www.wellplated.com/chocolate-oatmeal/#_a5y_p=3402284

9. http://www.niomismart.com/2015/09/5-what-i-eat-in-day-recipes.html?spref=pi

10. http://bojongourmet.com/2010/02/vegan-chocolate-coconut-milk-tapioca_14/

11. http://dineanddish.net/2014/05/double-chocolate-french-toast-recipe/

12. http://theprettybee.com/2015/09/vegan-pumpkin-chocolate-chip-pancakes.html

Bakes and Cakes

13. http://chocolatecoveredkatie.com/2011/11/06/one-minute-chocolate-cake/

14. http://dyingforchocolate.blogspot.com/2011/03/aunt-veras-chocolate-oatmeal-pie-sara.html

15. http://veganlovlie.com/2015/11/vegan-chocolate-pumpkin-loaf-cake-recipe.html

16. http://petiteallergytreats.com/bagels-gluten-free-chocolate-chip-egg-free/

17. http://www.popsugar.com/food/Vegan-Chocolate-Banana-Bread-36904908

18. http://www.glutenfreeveganpantry.com/chocolate-penaut-butter-chickpea-blondies-vegan-gluten-free/

19. http://simpleveganblog.com/simple-vegan-chocolate-chip-muffins/

20. http://chocolatechocolateandmore.com/chocolate-depression-cake/

21. http://fitfoodiefinds.com/2014/10/grain-free-biscotti/

22. http://iheartvegetables.com/2013/04/01/gluten-free-protein-donuts/

23. http://thebigmansworld.com/2015/10/05/healthy-3-ingredient-flourless-brownies/

24. http://www.countrycleaver.com/2015/02/gluten-free-mini-chocolate-orange-scones.html

25. http://avirtualvegan.com/double-chocolate-scones/

26. http://kitchenconfidante.com/double-dark-chocolate-zucchini-bread-recipe

27. http://www.wellplated.com/chocolate-chunk-coffee-muffins/

28. http://chocolatecoveredkatie.com/2014/10/14/avocado-chocolate-cake/

29. http://veganinthefreezer.com/mothers-chocolate-strudel/

30. http://minimalistbaker.com/vegan-chocolate-lava-cakes/

31. http://www.errenskitchen.com/no-bake-chocolate-oreo-cheesecake/

32. http://veganheaven.org/recipe/vegan-chocolate-hazelnut-donuts/

Cookies

33. http://www.food.com/recipe/chewy-vegan-chocolate-chocolate-chip-cookies-99094

34. http://www.texanerin.com/2013/04/chocolate-peanut-butter-macaroons.html

35. http://anunrefinedvegan.com/2015/06/12/flourless-peanut-butter-cookies-day-cookies-with-chocolate/

36. http://flippindelicious.com/2015/11/coconut-flour-cookies-gluten-free-grain-free-dairy-free-refined-sugar-free-egg-free.html

37. http://www.simplyquinoa.com/no-bake-chocolate-quinoa-cookies/

38. http://theviewfromgreatisland.com/double-dark-chocolate-shortbread-cookies/

39. http://theviewfromgreatisland.com/deepest-chocolate-espresso-chip-cookies/

40. http://pureella.com/two-ingredient-cookies-naturally-gluten-free-and-vegan/

41. http://www.adventures-in-cooking.com/2014/06/vegan-oreos-homemade-blendtec-coconut.html

Candies

42. http://sallysbakingaddiction.com/2012/04/24/3-ingredient-sugar-free-chocolate-bars-vegan/

43. http://minimalistbaker.com/2-ingredient-dark-chocolate-truffles/?utm_source=feedburner&utm_medium=feed&utm_campaign=Feed:+MinimalistBaker+%28Minimalist+Baker%29

44. http://chocolatecoveredkatie.com/2013/12/05/chocolate-jello-shots/

45. http://thevegan8.com/2014/04/21/cherry-jam-chocolate-cups/

45. http://www.chicvegan.com/recipe-pine-bark/

46. http://minimalistbaker.com/orange-almond-biscotti/

47. http://www.onegreenplanet.org/vegan-food/recipe-cadbury-creme-eggs/

48. http://www.the-girl-who-ate-everything.com/2015/01/potato-chip-popcorn.html

49. http://lorimerkitchen.com/2013/10/19/vegan-white-chocolate/

50. http://www.myrecipes.com/recipe/chocolate-almond-cherry-crisps

51. http://namelymarly.com/vegan-kit-kat-bars/

52. http://thevietvegan.com/vegan-peanut-butter-cups/

Fruits and Chocolate

53. http://chocolatecoveredkatie.com/2014/06/19/chocolate-covered-cherries/

54. http://ultimatechocolateblog.blogspot.com/

55. http://www.texanerin.com/2015/01/chocolate-raspberry-oat-bars.html#_a5y_p=3416943

56. http://anunrefinedvegan.com/2015/02/04/chocolate-apricot-truffle-chocolate-cups/

57. http://honestcooking.com/vegan-chocolate-dipped-strawberries/

58. http://www.runningwithspoons.com/2015/04/15/chocolate-chip-banana-bread-energy-bites/

59. http://www.myrecipes.com/recipe/chocolate-amaretti-peaches

Handy Snacks

60. http://ohsheglows.com/2010/05/17/3-ingredient-homemade-chocolate-covered-raisins/

61. http://ohsheglows.com/2013/07/29/super-seed-chocolate-protein-bites/

62. http://bakerbynature.com/healthy-greek-yogurt-chocolate-fudge-pops/

63. http://chocolatecoveredkatie.com/2015/10/08/chocolate-pumpkin-fudge-vegan-6-ingredients/

64. http://www.thekitchn.com/how-to-make-chocolatedipped-frozen-banana-bites-cooking-lessons-from-the-kitchn-201522

65. http://livetoeatit.com/dark-chocolate-coconut-balls/

Ice-Cream

66. http://thevegan8.com/2013/12/13/mocha-ice-cream/

67. http://www.thehealthymaven.com/2015/06/peanut-butter-chocolate-banana-soft-serve.html

68. http://ohsheglows.com/2014/03/28/the-big-vegan-banana-split/

Shakes and Smoothies

69. http://thefrugalgirls.com/2013/10/crockpot-hot-chocolate.html

70. http://www.purewow.com/entry_detail/recipe/10815/Frosty-mocha-milk-shakes.htm

71. http://www.briana-thomas.com/white-hot-chocolate/

72. http://www.healthysmoothiehq.com/chocolate-almond-avocado-smoothie

73. http://momtomomnutrition.com/food-and-recipes/chocolate-spinach-smoothie/

74. http://chocolatecoveredkatie.com/2014/08/04/cookie-dough-protein-shake/

75. http://www.theroastedroot.net/aphrodisiac-smoothie-with-cacao-and-maca/

76. http://www.godairyfree.org/recipes/mexican-chocolate-smoothie

77. http://anunrefinedvegan.com/2015/08/11/the-almond-milk-cookbook-chocolate-raspberry-smoothie/

78. http://www.theglowingfridge.com/post-workout-chocolate-peanut-butter-smoothie/

79. http://thealmondeater.com/2015/09/mint-chocolate-chip-smoothie/

80. http://thealmondeater.com/2015/04/almond-coconut-mocha-smoothie/

81. http://iheartvegetables.com/2015/10/02/chocolate-avocado-smoothie-vegan/

82. http://www.runningwithspoons.com/2016/02/02/chocolate-hemp-overnight-oatmeal-smoothie/

83. http://makethebestofeverything.com/2015/04/healthy-oreo-blizzard.html

Sauces, Syrups and Frostings

84. http://thevegan8.com/2013/10/25/the-ultimate-vegan-chocolate-glaze/

85. http://veggieprimer.com/dark-chocolate-avocado-frosting/

86. http://www.topwithcinnamon.com/2013/05/healthy-3-ingredient-chocolate-fudge-sauce-no-added-sugar-grain-free-vegan-gluten-free.html

87. http://www.smartnutrition.ca/recipes/diy-vegan-chocolate-syrup/

88. http://rawmanda.com/date-paste/

89. http://butyoucancallmecrazy.blogspot.com/2011/03/best-chocolate-sauce.html

90. http://www.makingthymeforhealth.com/2015/09/28/decadent-chocolate-fruit-dip/

91. http://detoxinista.com/creamy-cashew-icing-dairy-free/

No Bake Desserts

92. http://www.theglowingfridge.com/chocolate-covered-brownie-pops/

93. http://minimalistbaker.com/3-ingredient-dark-chocolate-peppermint-mousse/#_a5y_p=3240651

94. http://chocolatecoveredkatie.com/2015/06/25/healthy-chocolate-pudding-recipe/?utm_source=explorer.sheknows.com&utm_medium=referral&utm_campaign=ske_558c24340d2f37721e00000a

95. http://www.bakedbyrachel.com/egg-free-chocolate-chip-cookie-dough/

96. http://www.thetomatotart.com/recipe/gf-vegan-chocolate-peanut-butter-pie/

97. http://mywholefoodlife.com/2016/01/08/chocolate-pistachio-mousse/

98. http://www.theglowingfridge.com/no-bake-double-chocolate-brownie-bars/

99. http://theprettybee.com/2015/11/3-ingredient-dairy-free-fudge.html

100. http://www.veggieful.com/2012/10/vegan-chocolate-custard-recipe.html

101. http://www.myrecipes.com/recipe/peanut-butter-chocolate-pretzels

www.ingramcontent.com/pod-product-compliance
Lightning Source LLC
Chambersburg PA
CBHW071214080526
44587CB00013BA/1365